WOMEN
AND THEIR
JEWELS

15 iconic women through their jewellery

DAVID LELAIT-HELO

MITCHELL
BEAZLEY

Contents

INTRODUCTION
The Adorned Body
4

A CHILDLIKE PASSION FOR JEWELS
Elizabeth Taylor
10

SCANDALOUS JEWELLERY
Marie Antoinette
26

AN ARIA OF JEWELS
Maria Callas
38

AN EXCEPTIONAL COLLECTION OF 1960s JEWELLERY
Ava Gardner
52

JEWELLERY AS ARMOUR
Helena Rubinstein
60

THE JEWELS OF A DOWNFALL
Soraya
70

THE ART OF THE ACCESSORY
Jackie Kennedy Onassis
80

THE QUEEN OF JEWELS
Elizabeth II
90

AN OBSESSION WITH TIARAS
Barbara Hutton
108

ALL CHANGE FOR ROYAL JEWELLERY
Diana, Princess of Wales
122

THE LAST CROWN JEWELS
Eugénie de Montijo
136

THE JEWELS OF EXILE
The Duchess of Windsor
148

DIAMONDS ON THE RIVIERA
Grace Kelly
162

'HEAVENS, MY JEWELS!'
Begum Om Habibeh
174

ON THE ART OF SHINING IN SOCIETY
Brooke Astor
184

A panther bracelet by Cartier, 1952, one of the outstanding pieces in Wallis Simpson's jewellery collection. Jointed throughout, in platinum, diamonds and black onyx.

The Adorned Body

'The love of jewels is the most extreme form of materialism, an extreme form of love of matter, of the cult of the Earth. But it is a metaphysical materialism, for it is a way of recognising that the Earth and precious stones have the quality of God, of glory […] To the point that in order to prove our glory, elevate ourselves, demonstrate our social distinction, we have to cover our bodies with fruits of the Earth.'

EMANUELE COCCIA, 'LE BIJOU COMME OBJET D'ÉLÉVATION' IN *L'ÂME DU BIJOU* (PARIS: FLAMMARION, 2021), TRANS. *THE SOUL OF JEWELLERY* BY THE SAME PUBLISHER.

In 1912, the popular French song '*La femme aux bijoux*' (The Bejewelled Woman), with its accordion waltz rhythm, was on everyone's lips. In its lyrics, the woman of the title is both desired and feared: 'She is the bejewelled woman / She who makes people mad / She is beguiling / All who have loved her / Have suffered, have wept…' She fascinates as much as she bewitches. Her jewels give her her character and make her stand out from the crowd. The French word *bijou*, which first appeared around 1660, denoted 'a small finely crafted object used as an adornment'. It is thought to have come from the Celtic word *biz*, meaning finger, from which was derived the Breton term *bizou*, meaning a ring worn on the finger. A cognate word is the French word *joyau*, meaning jewel or gem, derived from Old French *joiel*, from which came *jeu* (game), *joie* (joy) and *jouissance* (enjoyment). Exquisite pleasure seems implicit to gems and jewellery, although, as we shall see, they also bring sorrow.

'I do think jewels, not jewellery, are very wonderful and extraordinary,' said the legendary fashion editor Diana Vreeland. 'I also wouldn't want only one jewel. I'd want a number…the biggest and the best quality.' For some women they are essential, to the point that they could not live without them. 'When I forget to put on jewellery, those close to me call the doctor, because they are sure I am ill,' the heiress and socialite Evalyn Walsh McLean wrote in her memoirs. And one of her most devoted followers, the actor Elizabeth Taylor, a famous champion of jewellery herself, created this axiom: 'Life isn't just about money, it's also about furs and jewellery' – jewellery which, all her life, she cherished, kissed and caressed, and with which she maintained a lifelong brilliant dialogue.

An intimate trophy par excellence, as close as can be to the skin and the blood, a jewel begins by adorning the body before taking on a great emotional charge, embodying true attachment. For the French novelist Laurence Cossé, jewellery is 'one of the heart's beautiful movements'. An item of jewellery is a symbol. At the same time as it satisfies a quest for power and an immutable desire to shine, it has been

An advertisement for the house of Van Cleef & Arpels by Jean-Gabriel Domergue, January 1923.

> 'I think that if one wanted to find the origin of jewellery, it would be necessary to go back almost to the creation of the world […] There is reason to presume that it was born of the desire to please, which is certainly not modern, and without which there would be no art, no industry, no charm in society; it is even said that we owe to it the discovery of fire. Such a useful gift fully deserves that we relate its history.'
>
> JEAN HENRI PROSPER POUGET, *TRAITÉ DES PIERRES PRÉCIEUSES* [TREATISE ON PRECIOUS STONES], 1762.

a sign of belonging since the dawn of time – to a social group, religion, generation, ethnicity or family. Through it we show not only our wealth and panache but also our power. Just as a bishop's ring is the mark of his ministry, Elizabeth II arranged her brooches depending on the diplomatic or sentimental message she wanted to convey.

Jewellery is passed on. It is a protection and a bond, even if but a modest one, between the generations, beyond time and death. Even if small, it can discreetly hold a high market value and thus enable the survival of a family in exile, or the salvation of a wronged woman. How many women, as humiliation or revolution was imminent, have hidden their gems in the hem of their skirt or the lining of their coat? But its value also makes jewellery vulnerable: ever at the mercy of historical upheavals and other reversals of fortune, a gem can be stolen, transformed, dismantled, removed from its setting, even melted. Thus, unlike furniture, sculptures or paintings, pieces of high jewellery are works of art that struggle to be passed on to posterity. Today, this makes them all the more exceptional – and oh so precious.

Conceived as an ideal jewellery collection, this book explores the relationship between fifteen famous women and their jewellery. Their beloved treasures implicitly bear the marks of love and exile, of both intimate dramas and brilliant victories. The fabulous jewels of Princess Soraya were the sparkling compensation for her terrible repudiation. Maria Callas used jewels to drive away the memories of her miserable childhood. Barbara Hutton, America's 'Poor Little Rich Girl', walked around with a tiara on her head and demanded she be addressed as 'Princess'. Elizabeth Taylor was the mistress of the art of starting a domestic quarrel so that presents of jewels might seal a reconciliation. Marie Antoinette was dishonoured by a diamond necklace … Here we peep into these women's collections and admire their sparkling jewellery close up – for beneath the gold and the precious stones beat their passionate and impatient hearts.

An extravagant gorgerin or drapery necklace in platinum and yellow gold, forming a lattice of emerald-cut amethysts, diamonds and turquoise gems, with a large heart-shaped amethyst in the centre, which belonged to the Duchess of Windsor.

Following pages: Part of a set of Triphane jewels by Van Cleef & Arpels, made of kunzite gems, amethysts and diamonds, which belonged to Elizabeth Taylor.

A CHILDLIKE PASSION FOR JEWELS

Elizabeth Taylor

'By the age of fifteen, I really did have a new love in my life: jewellery. And I've been loyal to that love ever since,' the actor once declared.[1] For Elizabeth Taylor, jewels were a devouring passion – a passion that built a legendary collection.

A violet gaze set with pearls. A scene from the movie *Ash Wednesday* by Larry Peerce, starring Elizabeth Taylor, Henry Fonda and Helmut Berger (1973).

On 13 and 14 December 2011, in New York City, eighty legendary pieces of jewellery were scattered to the four winds. The world's most famous jewellery houses, collectors and billionaires from the Middle East and Asia were waiting to pounce. Nine months after the death of the violet-eyed actor at the age of seventy-nine, her beloved jewels – historic pieces, unique creations and priceless gemstones alike – were, as she had expected, put up for auction by Christie's New York. A war chest … and a treasury of love. Each piece had an accompanying memory of a film shoot or a marriage, a reconciliation or a desire. No one treasured their jewellery collection more than Elizabeth Taylor. 'She liked to play with them, like a child plays with dolls,' said Ruth Peltason, who devoted a book to the actor's collection.[2] There was indeed an unbreakable bond between the star and her jewels: she caressed them, gazed at them and wore them all day long, even when she was in pyjamas or a tracksuit.

Elizabeth Taylor on the set of Vincente Minnelli's *The Sandpiper* (1965).

THE QUEEN OF HOLLYWOOD

If diamonds are a girl's best friend, Elizabeth Taylor quickly understood they are also the most beautiful gifts men can give. Her first two husbands – Nicky Hilton, heir to the luxury hotel chain, and Michael Wilding – barely responded to her discreet requests and chose to overlook her taste for clearing jewellers' cases. In 1950, when she first got engaged to Hilton, she nevertheless received a superb ring set with a 4-carat diamond. Her third husband, the theatre and film producer Mike Todd, had more of a feeling for gift-giving, and the young woman was ecstatic when he slipped onto her left ring finger an engagement ring set with an exceptional emerald-cut diamond of 29.40 carats.

A few months later, one fine day in August 1957, by the side of the swimming pool of a villa in Saint-Jean-Cap-Ferrat, Provence, the actor found herself covered with an avalanche of jewels. In the middle of the summer, Todd gave her a fabulous set of Cartier diamonds and rubies – a necklace, bracelet and earrings. A movie camera recorded the moment for posterity, and Elizabeth never looked more radiant. Todd did not stop there. 'You are my queen, and I think you should have a tiara,' he murmured, as he gave her a fabulous diamond tiara.[3] This kind of head jewellery had gone out of fashion, but she could not have cared less – playing the princess enchanted her. All her life she would wear a pair of diamond girandole earrings Todd had given her before he died in a plane crash on 22 March 1958.

Despite her grief, she soon found refuge in the arms of her late husband's best friend, the singer Eddie Fisher. The only snag was that her new lover was also the husband of Debbie Reynolds, an actor adored by the American public, who wasted no time in tearing into Miss Taylor, the country's number-one husband stealer. Nonetheless, Fisher left his wife and child to marry Elizabeth, sealing their relationship with a new suite of diamonds. Five years of marriage came to an end with the acquisition of a pair of earrings set with canary-yellow diamonds from the House of Bulgari – a gift that he hoped would win her back. By the time Fisher showed up in Rome to present them to Taylor – she was shooting *Cleopatra* with Richard Burton at the time – she had already succumbed to the manly charms of her co-star. When Fisher proffered the earrings, she barely looked at them and dismissed him there and then. Her vanquished husband retreated, but not without sending her the bill for them a few days later. Even so, Bulgari was a magic word for Taylor, a door opener in the actor's life. 'The only Italian word she knows is Bulgari,' Richard Burton quipped, before adding: 'I introduced her to beer, she introduced me to Bulgari.'[4]

A set of Cartier jewels in platinum, gold, diamonds and rubies (1951), given to Elizabeth Taylor by Mike Todd, her third husband. The necklace can also be worn as a tiara (top left).

A STONE'S THROW FROM THE BULGARI SHOP

In the eyes of the film's director, Joseph Mankiewicz, Elizabeth Taylor was the queen of Egypt, a divine Cleopatra. More than apt, then, that she should be involved in the most expensive movie in the history of the cinema up to that point. Within a year, the production was bogged down in mishaps and tantrums, beset with bad weather and management problems – not to mention a large lion that escaped from its cage. Nor would anyone ever forget the first filming sessions in London, where a fog so thick you could have cut it with a knife crept down the streets – hardly a setting evocative of pharaonic Egypt and not kind to Taylor's fragile airways either, causing her repeated bouts of bronchitis. Double pneumonia even led to a tracheotomy, after which exhaustion confined her to a wheelchair.

Finally, it was possible to resume shooting – first in California, then in Rome, where the star completely recovered her health. In a mild Roman January, surrounded by pasteboard scenery depicting the ancient city, Taylor prepared to say her first lines to Mark Antony, played by the Welshman Richard Burton. She wore a yellow dress that her amethyst eyes lit up; she was more radiant than ever. Burton, clad in thick leather, his face lined and his complexion somewhat clouded by the previous evening's excessive alcohol intake, was hardly vigorous. 'He was hungover and very vulnerable and his hands were shaking,' Taylor said later. 'He asked me to hold a coffee cup up to his lips, and I was gone.'[5] Love at first sight was inevitable and earth-shaking: it was Beauty and the Beast, two volcanic temperaments united in an embrace. Right away, Taylor showed her new love the way to the Bulgari shop …

The first time, Burton thought he would be shelling out for a modest present priced at $100,000. The couple were shown some small earrings, but they were immediately pushed aside as Taylor had already spotted an indecently large necklace. This marvel was made up of diamonds and seventeen emeralds, one of which was a pendant of almost 24 carats, detachable so it could also be worn as a brooch. Burton signed an eye-watering cheque. In subsequent years, Taylor's collection of jewellery expanded to lavish proportions. Bought back by Bulgari in 2011 for $6.1 million, the necklace was worn in 2013 by the actor Julianne Moore, as the face of Bulgari.

A fabulous set of emerald and diamond jewels by Bulgari, the first pieces of which were bought by Richard Burton in Rome during the filming of *Cleopatra* in 1962.

IN SEARCH OF THE WORLD'S MOST BEAUTIFUL JEWELS

With their respective spouses now summarily dismissed, the intrepid lovers could adore each other in plain sight. On 15 March 1964, Elizabeth Taylor and Richard Burton were married in Suite 810 of the Ritz in Montreal. There followed an international bohemian life, as they went from luxury hotel to palace, never accompanied by less than 400kg (about 900lb) of luggage. They loved each other furiously, in a clamour of huge rages, a conflagration of passionate embraces, a fog of alcohol. When a break-up threatened, Burton reconquered his sweetheart by unearthing diamonds as big as wine corks; Taylor then felt adored and she exulted in seeing her jewellery case filled with a few new trinkets. For Burton, this was the start of a mad quest for diamonds, just to see the wonder shining in his beloved's lilac eyes.

For the sake of love, the rough-and-ready Welshman came to frequent the hushed rooms of jewellers as well as the noisier confines of auction houses. One of his biggest finds, in May 1968 at Parke Bernet in New York, was the Krupp Diamond (now known as the Elizabeth Taylor Diamond) – an absolutely pure, D-colour gem of 33.19 carats, which he bought for $300,000 dollars. This ring had previously belonged to Vera Krupp, the heiress of 'the famous munitions family which helped knock off millions of Jews', as Taylor wrote later in *Elizabeth Taylor: My Love Affair with Jewelry*. 'I though how perfect it would be if a nice Jewish girl like me were to own it.'[6] Never, not even after her two divorces from Burton, did she remove this diamond – not even in the bath. 'It's practical – it goes with everything!' she joked.[7] The gem elicited a caustic quip from Princess Margaret: 'It's so big, it's almost vulgar!' 'Isn't it?' the actor contented herself with replying, as the solitaire

Elizabeth Taylor proudly displays one of the many tokens of love given to her by the Welsh actor Richard Burton. Here, the Krupp diamond of 33.19 carats, which she never took off.

A creation by the American David Webb. Two strands of fine pearls fastened by a clasp consisting of two lions' heads encrusted with diamonds and emeralds, 1965.

Michael Jackson, a prodigious friend

He was not a husband, nor even a lover, but simply the best friend in the world. 'No one can imagine how much we loved each other ... It was the most beautiful relationship of my life... My life is so empty now,' Taylor declared after the death of the King of Pop — she was the first to call him by that nickname.[8] Their friendship began in 1984 after she attended a concert he gave at the Dodger Stadium in Los Angeles. On learning that she had slipped away before the end of the show, Michael Jackson had burst into tears, and then called her to ask the reason for her early departure. She replied that she had not been able to see or hear him very well. There followed three hours of conversation on all manner of subjects. It was a *coup de foudre*, as they themselves later described the encounter.

From then on they were inseparable, appearing hand in hand on red carpets and at Hollywood parties. The King of Pop paid homage to his friend, singing 'Elizabeth, I Love You' on the evening of the party for her sixty-fifth birthday. Those twenty-five years of friendship were punctuated by fabulous gifts given by the singer to his adored star: two diamond watches, a ring set with a 17-carat pear-shaped sapphire, yellow diamond pendants, a clip shaped like a bow studded with diamonds by Van Cleef & Arpels, and also a most singular set of jewels: a necklace and earrings encrusted with diamonds and coloured precious stones depicting little monkeys — Jackson's favourite animal. This suite, bought by the singer in 2000 at a Christie's sale, came from the collection of the Baron and Baroness of Portanova.

Necklace and earrings in diamonds, emeralds and gold by Massoni, depicting monkeys and a profusion of bananas. A gift from Michael Jackson.

covered her ring finger with a thousand sparkles.[8] In 2011, it was bought by a South Korean conglomerate for the astronomical sum of $8.8 million.

A HISTORIC PEARL WORN BY MARY TUDOR

The treasure hunt continued. One day, the lovers played table tennis in Gstaad not for points but for diamonds. Taylor won every time and carried off three solitaires. Burton played along. A few months later, in January 1969, it was a pearl that excited her covetousness – the 203-grain Peregrina that had once belonged to the kings of Spain. It was discovered in the Gulf of Panama by an enslaved African in the sixteenth century and given to the King of Spain, Philip II, who kept it for his future wife, Mary Tudor, Queen of England.

For more than two centuries, the pearl, mounted in a brooch, was worn by successive Spanish queens, before leaving the country in 1808 when Joseph Bonaparte, the brother of Napoleon I who had been installed as king of Spain, fled, his pockets stuffed with the crown jewels. Joseph subsequently gave the pearl to his nephew, the future Napoleon III, who sold it to James Hamilton, future 1st Duke of Abercorn. The pearl, ever wayward, was mislaid twice, lost in the cushions of a Windsor Castle sofa and later on the wooden floor of the Buckingham Palace ballroom. The Hamiltons sold it at auction in 1969. Burton pipped a grandson of King Alfonso XIII to the post and carried off the precious pearl for $37,000. He gave it to Taylor for her thirty-seventh birthday. In order to showcase this precious gift, she asked Cartier to create a Renaissance-style necklace made up of pearls, diamonds and rubies.

This pearl was to give her a terrible fright. One day, when she was filming in Las Vegas, she thought she had lost it. Eventually, she found it in the mouth of her Pekinese, who had mistaken it for a bone.

The final design for a necklace by Cartier in 1972 intended to showcase a historic pearl, the Peregrina. Platinum, diamonds, rubies and pearls.

The Peregrina, worn by Elizabeth Taylor on 19 January 1992 in Los Angeles.

THE TAJ MAHAL DIAMOND – THE ULTIMATE TOKEN OF LOVE

On 25 December 1968, again in Gstaad, a Christmas stocking made Taylor's heart beat faster. She did not immediately discern, among the sweets, a small box stamped with the name Van Cleef & Arpels. 'I think I fainted,' she would say years later when describing the fabulous 8.24-carat ruby Burton gave her. He had indeed gone in search of the most beautiful ruby in the world – no doubt to vie with the set of rubies once bought for her by Eddie Fisher. This exceptional ruby, mounted on a yellow gold ring and set alongside eight brilliant-cut diamonds, would be sold for $3 million in 2011 – three times the original estimate.

The birth of Taylor's first grandchild in 1971 was also the occasion for an exceptional gift from Burton: the Barquerolles Lion Necklace, featuring a lion's head and navette-cut diamonds. It was an ingenious item of jewellery, as the choker could be converted into two bracelets, while the lion's head, with its emerald eyes, was detachable and could be used as a clip. The House of Van Cleef & Arpels bought back its creation in 2011 for $900,000, or almost six times its estimate.

As long as the couple's tumultuous love affair continued, crazier and crazier gifts came one after the other. Among these was a sumptuous Bulgari Art Deco sautoir necklace featuring a cabochon sapphire of 52.77 carats. After it had been bought back by the house that had designed it, it reappeared around the neck of the actor Jessica Chastain in 2013. Even more precious – and symbolic – was the Taj Mahal Diamond, a flat stone engraved with Mogul inscriptions, acquired by Burton in 1972. Its origin was the stuff of legend: in the early seventeenth century, it had supposedly been given by the Mogul emperor

The Taj Mahal, set with a flat, engraved diamond — the most famous of love tokens, given around 1600 by the Mogul emperor Shah Jahan to Mumtaz, his beloved wife. Richard Burton bought it in 1972.

The Duchess of Windsor, a rival in jewellery

Elizabeth Taylor was a woman who had the means to satisfy her voracious appetite for jewels. At a Sotheby's auction held on 2 April 1987, she coveted a piece belonging to the Duchess of Windsor, that other famous devourer of diamonds: it was lot 27, a brooch consisting of three plumes of diamonds, the coat of arms of the Prince of Wales. This jewel symbolized the abdication of Edward VIII and his willingness to do anything out of love for Wallis Simpson. Sotheby's even declined to include an image of the jewel in its catalogue, for fear of upsetting the sensibilities of the queen, as this subject remained potentially explosive at the Palace. Rumour had it that the royal family, or even the queen herself, might bid. But this did not take into account the tenacity of Elizabeth Taylor. Indeed, in her eyes this jewel was a homage to Richard Burton, who had died three years earlier. She was all the more determined because, on once meeting the duchess wearing the clip, the latter had told her she could have a copy made — a suggestion Taylor, needless to say, refused. Copies were absolutely not for her.

Picture the star, lounging by her swimming pool and firing off her outrageous bids into the telephone receiver, surrounded by the children and grandchildren she had invited over for the occasion. The figures soared: Taylor was not letting go. She wanted this brooch, and got it for 850,000 Swiss francs. 'I let out a great scream. The children did too, especially when I told them the price. Some of them jumped in the pool,' she later recalled.[9]

Twenty-four years later, after Taylor had died, her children, respecting her last wishes, announced that the most fabulous jewel collection of the twentieth century would be sold at Christie's. It was discovered that each piece had its own case, accompanied by a label giving its provenance and history. Like a pop star, the collection went off on a global tour, before being dispersed for ever at auction, attaining a total of $137 million — a record for a jewellery sale.

A brooch made up of three plumes of diamonds, a heraldic symbol of the Princes of Wales, which belonged to the Duchess of Windsor and was bought by Elizabeth Taylor in 1987.

Shah Jahan to his beloved wife Mumtaz, after whose death he commissioned the famous white marble mausoleum, the Taj Mahal, to be built on the banks of the Ganges. In 2011, the Taj Mahal diamond necklace was sold for $8.8 million.

Apart from these exceptional pieces, Richard Burton gave his wife numerous everyday jewels, such as the Van Cleef sautoir necklaces she adored, the Triphanes model in yellow gold, set with kunzites, diamonds and amethysts (the colour of her eyes), and the Dodecanese, Panka, Lamartine, Pompon and Ibiza collections, adorned with coral, diamond and amethyst cabochons.

Finally worn out, the couple divorced in 1974, before remarrying in October 1975 and once again ending the marriage a few months later. Elizabeth Taylor would be married eight times, with each new union accompanied by a few new jewels. But none of these subsequent husbands would be gripped by the acquisitive frenzy that took hold of Burton, always Taylor's great love. When a journalist asked whether her husbands were embarrassed when she wore the gifts of their predecessors, and especially those of Richard Burton, she replied with a smiling no, adding that, on the contrary, in doing so she only encouraged them to give her even bigger ones.

Barquerolles necklace with a lion's head and matching ear pendants by Van Cleef & Arpels — yellow gold, emeralds, and diamonds, 1971. This jewel can be converted into two bracelets, and the pendant can be detached and worn as a clip. It was given to Elizabeth Taylor by Richard Burton in 1971, on the birth of her first grandchild. Design for the Barquerolles necklace, 1971. Van Cleef & Arpels Archives.

A 1970s sautoir necklace by Bulgari in platinum, sapphires and diamonds. The pendant, set with a cabochon sapphire, can also be worn as a brooch. It was bought by the House of Bulgari at the historic sale of Elizabeth Taylor's jewels in 2011.

The Burton–Taylor Diamond

Always on the lookout for big jewellery sales, Richard Burton never stopped aiming for the stars to take his beloved by surprise. In the autumn of 1969, an exceptional pear-shaped diamond of 69.42 carats, made from an uncut stone of 240.8 carats discovered in a South African mine three years earlier, caught his interest. This colossal stone was initially bought in 1967 by Harriet Annenberg Ames, who had it mounted on a ring, flanked by two smaller stones. Uncomfortable displaying such a jewel on the streets of Manhattan, its owner eventually decided to part with it, only two years after having bought it. This sale did not fail to excite Miss Taylor, who had the jewel brought to Switzerland so she could take a better look at it.

In New York, on 23 October 1969, the bidding was fierce: in the running were the jeweller Harry Winston, the shipping magnate Aristotle Onassis and the Sultan of Brunei. While Burton set himself a limit of $1 million, Robert Kenmore, head of the Kenmore Corporation, which then owned the New York branch of Cartier, prevailed, outbidding him by $50,000. Nevertheless, the next day, Burton — disinclined to concede defeat — bought the stone from Cartier for $1.1 million. Never before had a diamond attained such a record price.

The sale agreement stipulated that the diamond be exhibited in Cartier's shops in Chicago and New York before Taylor would take possession of it. No fewer than six thousand people a day flocked to look at this marvel, which the jeweller had in the meantime mounted on an equally impressive diamond rivière. Finally, a few days later, on 12 November 1969, at the Scorpio Ball held on the fortieth birthday of Princess Grace of Monaco, Taylor could proudly sport her necklace. Nine years later, Taylor nevertheless took a surprising decision: she put the diamond up for sale. The jeweller Henry Lambert offered $5 million. She devoted some of that sum to building a hospital in Botswana, the country where she had married Burton for the second time, in 1975. In 1979, Lambert in turn sold the diamond to one of his colleagues, Robert Mouawad.

On 7 April 1970, at the 42nd Oscars ceremony, Elizabeth Taylor wore a necklace of pear-shaped diamonds that featured, as a pendant, the famous Burton-Taylor diamond, a gem of 69.42 carats mounted by Cartier. This jewel, bought by Richard Burton in 1969 for $1.1 million, is now valued at $70 million.

SCANDALOUS JEWELLERY

Marie Antoinette

A queen who was despised in her day but who has become a revered icon two and a half centuries later, Marie Antoinette wore pearls and diamonds like no other sovereign – a self-indulgence that would eventually help bring about her own demise.

A portrait of Queen Marie Antoinette by Jean-Baptiste André Gautier d'Agoty, 1775. Her hair is adorned with strands of pearls and an imposing diamond motif.

On 14 November 2018, the hammer came down in a Geneva auction house. The auditorium, filled with buyers from forty-three countries, held its breath. *Sold – for €33 million!* The bidding contest, between a European collector and another from the Middle East, was worthy of the record books. The European had just prevailed. Up for auction was a very large pear-shaped natural saltwater pearl mounted on a pendant: the slightly baroque pearl itself 18mm (¾in) long, perfectly white and weighing 250 grains, and suspended from a modest bow encrusted with diamonds. Fabulous in itself, this piece becomes doubly so when one imagines it around the neck of Marie Antoinette, attached to a necklace consisting of six strands of pearls.

Nine other jewels that had belonged to the last queen of France before the French Revolution were offered for sale on the same day. Most were bought over the telephone by one buyer, the anonymous European: a pair of diamond and pearl earrings, a diamond brooch enhanced by a yellow diamond pendant, a single-stranded pearl necklace, a monogrammed ring containing a lock of the queen's hair, and another set with diamonds bearing at its centre a miniature of Marie Antoinette – the last two pieces being examples of the *bijoux de sentiment* that were very fashionable in the eighteenth century. In all, there were ten pieces from the Bourbon-Parma collection. Two centuries earlier, Marie Antoinette's eldest child, Marie-Thérèse de France – known as Madame Royale – had bequeathed a third of her jewellery collection to her niece and adopted daughter, Louise Marie Thérèse d'Artois, the Duchess of Parma.

Marie Antoinette having been elevated to the rank of pop icon by fashion and cinema, each of her jewels was regarded as a relic, hence the astronomical figure attained by the auction – €37.9 million. Three years later, also in Geneva, two diamond bracelets were snapped up for €7 million. Each had three strands and 112 cushion-cut diamonds; Marie Antoinette had acquired them in the summer of 1776 for 162,660 livres, after which she had to ask the king to settle the invoice sent by Charles Auguste Boehmer, the jeweller who, nine years later, would help drag the Crown into the notorious Affair of the Diamond Necklace.

In this painting by Élisabeth Louise Vigée-Lebrun, Marie Antoinette wears one of the many sets of pearls to which she was deeply attached.

A set of jewels that belonged to Marie Antoinette, sold at auction by the House of Bourbon-Parma in autumn 2018 — seen here on display in New York, 12 October 2018.

THE BEST-FURNISHED JEWELLERY CASE IN EUROPE

Marie Antoinette was just fourteen years old when, on 16 May 1770, she married the dauphin, Louis, in the Royal Chapel in Versailles. After centuries of conflict between France and Austria, Empress Maria Theresa of Austria had handed over her youngest daughter to the grandson of King Louis XV, with a view to reconciling the two royal houses.

As part of the marriage celebrations in Paris, a jubilant public filled the Place Louis XV – the future Place de la Concorde where, two decades later, the royal couple would be guillotined – only for the day to end in disaster when a fire broke out nearby and the consequent stampede led to the deaths of hundreds of people. An omen for the terrified young couple, surely, of the tragedies to come.

At Versailles, a royal household ruled by rigorous, merciless etiquette, Marie Antoinette was thrown in at the deep end. While she was hurt by the lack of intimacy and goodwill shown to her, this elegant young woman could however soon boast that she owned the finest jewellery collection anyone could ever have dreamed of. As well as the many jewels her mother had given her before she left Austria for France – notably diamonds and pearls worth half a million gold francs – on her arrival in Paris, Marie Antoinette also received the entire jewellery collection of her late mother-in-law, Maria Josepha of Saxony. This consisted of countless emerald and diamond jewels, rubies, strands of pearls,

A pendant of a pearl and diamonds attached to a three-strand pearl necklace, on display in London, 19 October 2018.

Brooch with a double ribbon of diamonds belonging to Queen Marie Antoinette, sold at auction 14 November 2018 in Geneva.

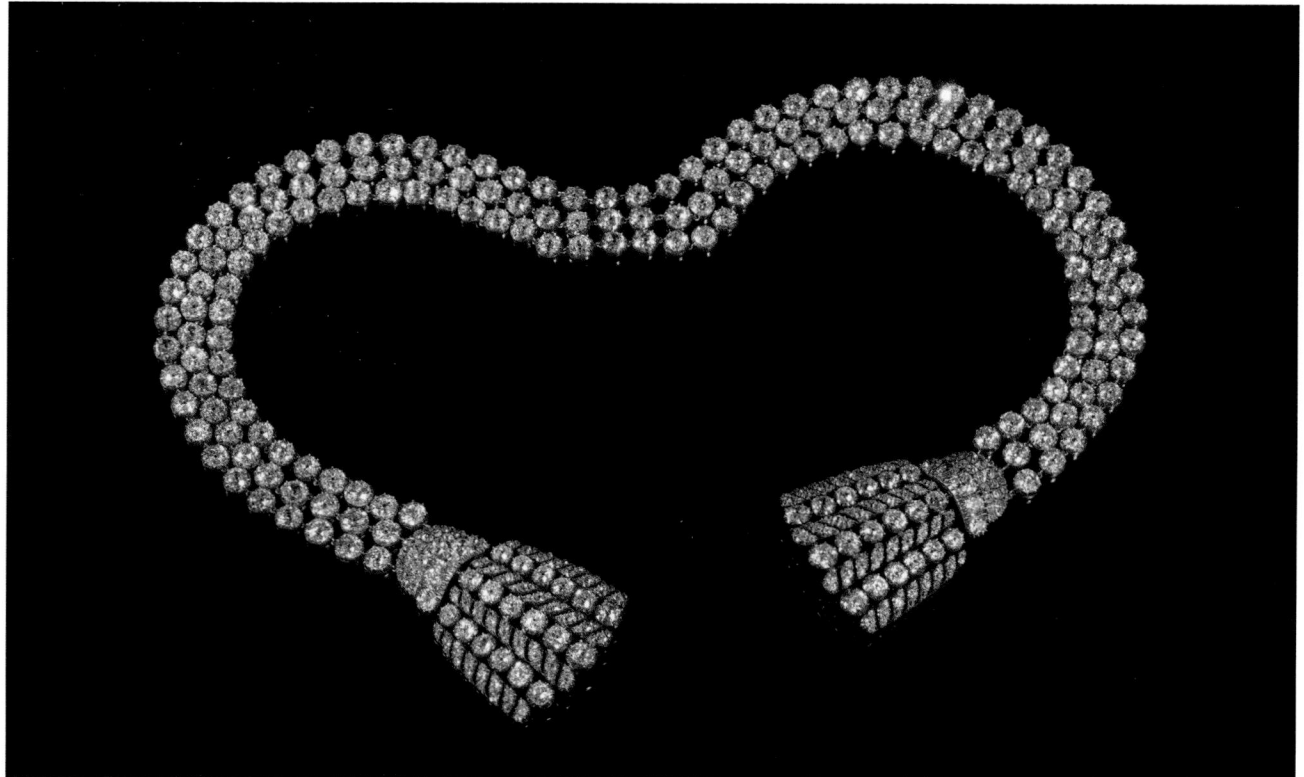

shoe buckles, a pair of fabulous girandole earrings and, above all, an imposing parure that included an extravagant stomacher and collection of brooches that were indispensable for securing the multiple flounces, ribbons and frills of the billowing dresses then in fashion.

Four years later, on the death of Louis XV in 1774, Louis XVI ascended the throne and, at the age of eighteen, Marie Antoinette became queen of France. Her extravagant taste in fashion, and especially in jewellery, led her to acquire vast numbers of new jewels even though this meant incurring heavy debts, while the king had to manage a state whose coffers were dangerously depleted. Among these gems was an extraordinary set of rubies, the queen's favourite precious stone, that came from the Crown's jewel collection and was valued at three million livres – a colossal sum at the time. She was also fond of pearls, wearing them around her neck, on her wrists and also as hair ornaments, wrapped up in her ringlets and locks, often combined with diamond headdresses of oriental design. Marie Antoinette possessed such a quantity of jewellery that, in 1787, she asked the cabinetmaker Jean-Ferdinand Schwerdfeger to make a *serre-bijoux* (jewellery safe) to house her collection. It was 2.63m (8ft 7½in) high, 2m (6ft 5¾in) wide and 65cm (2ft 1½in) deep. This monumental piece of furniture of unprecedented luxury was made from the finest mahogany, covered in bronze decorations and cameos, and encrusted with mother-of-pearl and Sèvres porcelain. Today, it can still be admired in the Queen's Bedroom in the Palace of Versailles.

The origin of this jewel, with 300 carats of diamonds, remains uncertain, but it is believed that some of its gems supposedly came from the famous jewel connected to the scandal of the Affair of the Diamond Necklace.

HER JEWELS ON THE WAY TO EXILE

The woman who was contemptuously nicknamed 'The Austrian' or 'Madame Deficit' would never find a place in the heart of the French people. Hostile pamphlets and bawdy songs tarnished her reputation from the very first few months of her reign. Marie Antoinette was called lecherous, frivolous, greedy and dishonest – as well as, quite wrongly, a spy for her native Austria – and was reproached for her extravagance and even her lack of piety. Feeling like a prisoner in the hothouse of Versailles, she sought refuge in a corner of its estates, at the Petit Trianon, a chateau Louis XV had had built for his mistress Madame de Pompadour and to which Louis XVI now gave his wife its diamond-encrusted key. To this sanctuary she added the Hameau de la Reine (Queen's Hamlet) – an idealized farm, complete with its own dairy and charming cottages. Swapping her heavy court clothes for a white percale dress, headscarf and straw hat, Marie Antoinette played at being a shepherdess, strolling carefree and happy among the real farmers and milkmaids, sheep, cows and pigs.

Much of the population of France, meanwhile, was starving, and rebellion was brewing. From the opening of the States-General – the country's legislative and consultative assembly – on 5 May 1789, the monarchy was called into question and the queen criticized. Marie Antoinette insisted that Louis XVI take action and move their family away from Paris, but it was already too late. They were soon forced to leave Versailles for the Tuileries Palace in Paris. She hastily burned her correspondence, while also seeing to the safekeeping of her jewels – her most valuable possessions. For this, the queen called on the assistance of Florimond Claude, Count of Mercy-Argenteau, the Austrian ambassador to France and her most faithful ally since her arrival in France.

According to legend, in 1780, outside the gates of the Palace of Versailles, the young jeweller Jean-Baptiste Mellerio offered to sell the queen this bracelet, consisting of garnets and seven cameos. It was one of the only jewels in Marie Antoinette's possession when she was detained in the Temple prison.

Under threat since the start of the Revolution, he had already moved his embassy to Brussels. In her memoirs, Madame Campan, the queen's chambermaid, described what happened: 'Her Majesty had, with me, settled into a mezzanine room that looked out on to the Tuileries gardens. We packed everything she owned in the way of diamonds, rubies, and pearls into a small box.'[10] She kept only a suite of pearls and some unmounted gems. The queen's treasure was sent to Mercy-Argenteau in Belgium, where it spent some time shut away in a vault before being sent on to the Austrian court. In March 1794, some six months after Marie Antoinette had been guillotined, an inventory of her jewels was made in Vienna in the presence of Archduke Charles, Duke of Teschen, the head of the Austrian army. Wrapped up in cotton cloth were numerous parures of diamonds, pearls, rubies and emeralds, but also some ruby, pearl, and emerald gemstones that had been formerly sewn onto the heels of the queen's shoes, to match the colour of her ensemble.

However, a few of Marie Antoinette's jewels took a different route – to England. Two years earlier, in 1792, after the royal couple's failed flight to Varennes, Marie Antoinette was imprisoned in the Les Feuillants Convent in Paris. With neither clothes nor money, she was dependent on the charity of her few friends, one of whom was Elizabeth Leveson-Gower, 19th Countess of Sutherland and wife of the British ambassador. When the countess brought the queen some fresh linen, the queen slipped her a small bag containing her very last pearls and diamonds, in the hope that she would one day retrieve them. This small treasure waited in vain for half a century, before being used to make a necklace for the wife of the countess's grandson in 1849. This piece, made of rubies and diamonds and embellished with twenty-one pear-shaped and twelve round grey pearls, was auctioned in 2007.

This necklace was made in 1849 by the Leveson-Gower family from pearls entrusted personally to Lady Sutherland by Marie Antoinette, in recognition of her helping her flee to Varennes during the night of 20–21 June 1791.

TOTAL FASCINATION

In December 1795 Emperor Francis II of Austria, Marie Antoinette's nephew, welcomed Marie-Thérèse of France, known as Madame Royale, the eldest daughter of Marie Antoinette and Louis XVI, to the Hofburg, his palace in Vienna. Then aged seventeen, she was now the sole survivor of the French royal family. Not without emotion, he handed her the small box containing her mother's jewels, some of which she immediately had to sell in order to pay for her own upkeep – notably a ruby parure that was bought by the Austrian emperor himself. Once dismantled, these gems became part of a new suite, worn some decades later by Empress Elisabeth of Austria, the famous Sisi, before they disappeared in the theft of the Habsburg jewels at the start of the twentieth century. Having become Duchess of Angoulême through her marriage to her cousin Louis-Antoine d'Artois, Madame Royale died childless in 1851, at the age of seventy-three. Three heirs – her nephew, the Count of Chambord, his wife and his sister, the Duchess of Parma, whom she had adopted – shared her estate equally, notably her very fine jewellery collection. From the end of the nineteenth century and throughout the twentieth, as a result of bankruptcies and various inheritances, several of these jewels featured in major jewellery auctions: in 1891, some pear-shaped diamonds mounted in earrings; in 1906, pendant earrings with pear-shaped pearls and diamonds; in 1928, a diadem and necklace in rubies and diamonds; and in 1951, a gold and white enamel jewel. More recently, in 2018 ten items of jewellery that had remained in the possession of the House of Bourbon-Parma for two centuries were sold, followed in 2021 by two diamond bracelets. The sums attained were ever more astronomical, in keeping with the glory of a martyred queen who has never ceased to inspire literature and films, fashion and cosmetics, and even video games, cartoons and a Japanese manga series that sold millions of copies, *The Rose of Versailles*.

In 2021, Christie's offered for sale these two bracelets commissioned by Marie Antoinette from the jeweller Charles Auguste Boehmer in 1776. Three strands of diamonds each, 112 old-cut gems — the smallest ones one carat, the biggest ones four. They could be combined and worn as a necklace.

Madame Royale, Duchess of Angoulême, in 1816, wearing on each wrist the bracelets of her mother, Queen Marie Antoinette. These were among the jewels secretly sent to Austria.

Marie Antoinette

The Affair of the Diamond Necklace

The historian Thomas Carlyle described the necklace in question thus: 'a row of seventeen glorious diamonds, as large almost as filberts [hazelnuts] [...] a three-wreathed festoon, and pendants enough (simple pear-shaped, multiple star-shaped, or clustering amorphous) encircle it [...] around a very Queen of Diamonds.'[11] 'A glorious ornament,' boasted the jewellers Charles Auguste Boehmer and Paul Bassenge, who had mortgaged the entirety of their assets in order to pay for the gems necessary to make such a jewel. Only a king could have afforded this piece, whose value was the equivalent of four luxurious châteaux. As Louis XV had died before Boehmer and Bassenge were able to offer it to him, the new Queen of France, Marie Antoinette, became their next target. She became their client in 1776, buying a pair of earrings and two diamond bracelets that Louis XVI paid for at his wife's request. The years passed, the necklace remained unsold, and the two jewellers found themselves in dire straits — so they took advantage of the birth of the first two royal children to offer their masterpiece to the king and queen. The response was a polite refusal, the queen observing that France had more need of ships than of diamond necklaces.

At that point, the century's most extraordinary fraud was hatched. In 1784, Jeanne de Valois-Saint-Remy, the self-styled 'Countess de La Motte' and supposedly descended from an illegitimate son of Henri II, appeared on the scene. Having noticed that the powerful Cardinal de Rohan, who had fallen from grace, was trying to win the queen's favour, she assured him she was close to her and would plead his case. The adventuress initiated a false correspondence between the prelate and the queen. Rohan took the bait and was now prepared to agree to all demands of the person he thought was the queen. Months passed, before a missive supposedly from the queen asked him to buy in her name, but in the utmost secrecy, a fabulous diamond necklace. An appointment was made, and Boehmer and Bassenge handed over the jewel to the prelate, who in turn consigned it to a supposed guard of the royal house. A few hours later, Jeanne de la Motte, her husband, and her lover were already removing the stones from their mountings using files and knives. The biggest ones were sold off in London, the rest under the table in Paris.

Scandal erupted when Boehmer, who was impatient by nature, went to Versailles to demand the first of four payments of 400,000 livres that had been promised to him — the jewel's price having been set at 1.6 million livres, or 13,000 years of a worker's wages. The affair created an uproar. On 15 August 1785, at the queen's request, the Cardinal de Rohan was arrested in the Hall of Mirrors in the presence of the entire court. The Church and nobility rose up in protest, before a trial cleared the prelate's name and condemned Jeanne de La Motte. Marie Antoinette, despite her innocence, saw her reputation tarnished yet again. The people were fascinated by this spectacular fraud and were convinced it was another of the queen's machinations. She was even accused of having offered her favours to the cardinal in exchange for the necklace. The affair, of course, gave credence to all the pamphlets, slander and rumours of which she was already the target. 'The case of the Necklace,' observed the Count of Mirabeau, 'was the prelude to the Revolution.'

A replica of the famous 'Queen's Necklace' created by the jewellers Paul Bassenge and Charles Auguste Boehmer.

AN ARIA OF JEWELS

Maria Callas

The archetypal diva, Maria Callas left a mark on the
twentieth century with both her singing and her elegance.
She was as famous for her gorgeous stage jewellery
as she was for the lavish pieces she wore in real life.

Maria Callas in Paris during the 1960s.

'Are there those who dare/To raise seditious voices, Warlike voices, before the altar of God.'[12] It was with these stirring words from Vincenzo Bellini's opera *Norma* that, on 19 December 1958, Maria Callas appeared on the stage of the Paris Opéra. This gala, held in the presence of the French president René Coty, was billed as 'the greatest show in the world', bringing together all of fashionable Paris – Jean Cocteau, Charlie Chaplin, Brigitte Bardot on the arm of Sacha Distel, Gilbert Bécaud and many more. The gold-and-crimson velvet of the auditorium glittered with the jewellery of the elegant women present – the rubies and diamonds of the Duchess of Windsor, the turquoise cabochons of Begum Aga Khan, the emeralds of Princess Maria Pia of Savoy … As she took centre stage, however, Maria Callas eclipsed them all. With a perfect chignon and eyelids painted midnight blue, dressed in deep red, her bare shoulders graced by a stole and her hand on her heart, she lit up the theatre with her brilliant presence.

Her regal jewels shimmered in the shadows – a diamond rivière necklace and pendant earrings consisting of two enormous pear-shaped diamonds, on loan from the House of Van Cleef & Arpels to the most venerated opera singer of the century. With her performances of '*Casta Diva*', the great aria from *Norma*, followed by arias from *Il Trovatore* and *The Barber of Seville*, and finally Act II of *Tosca*, with renowned baritone Tito Gobbi, Callas dispelled the scandal that had erupted in Rome in January of that year when, in the presence of the Italian president, her voice had failed her while singing the role of Norma at the Teatro dell'Opera and she had walked out of the performance after the first act. Later, an angry crowd gathered outside her hotel, and she was booed, insulted, cursed. The legend of the diva, gifted but temperamental, was born.

HER FIRST TROPHY: A WATCH

No one in the world saw Maria Anna Cecilia Sophia Kalogeropoulos coming. Not even her parents who, on 2 December 1923, were hoping for a son to replace a child who had died. She was born in New York to Greek immigrants whose hopes of making a fortune had remained unrealized. To make the family name more manageable, her father first shortened it to Kalos and later changed it to Callas. Five weeks would pass before Maria's mother, Evangelia, would even go near her strapping 5½kg (12lb) baby.

Evangelia's life was marked by frustration – she had dreamed of becoming a singer and marrying a rich man, while her actual husband, George, was just a small-time pharmacist whom the 1929 Wall Street Crash had made a little poorer still. As Maria grew up, she became fat, unlike her sister, Jackie, who was slender and graceful. In her awkward adolescence, acne and thick glasses disfigured Maria's chubby face, but what she did have was her agile and powerful voice, which got her noticed and captured even her mother's attention. Whenever Maria sang the popular song '*La Paloma*', Evangelia would brighten a little. Singing offered Maria redemption, too, and seemed to bring her the love she so badly wanted. A singing contest on the radio saw her win first prize and she received her first piece of jewellery: a modest watch that the proud Evangelia showed off in front of all the neighbours. This embittered woman went on to become a classic domineering stage mother, who made the budding young singer into a little performing monkey whom she exhibited shamelessly.

WITH EACH NEW OPERA, A SET OF JEWELS

Maria Callas was still an unknown when, in 1947, she arrived in Verona to sing the title role in Amilcare Ponchielli's opera *La Gioconda* in the Arena. Her manner was gauche and her body shapeless; nevertheless, Battista Meneghini, a lover of lyrical opera and wealthy entrepreneur, took her under his wing, later saying that he had felt a kind of compassion for the young opera singer. Callas asked only to love and be loved, and surrendered helplessly to a man who was twenty-seven years her senior. The letters she wrote him show her vulnerability and submissiveness. Despite his wealth, her mentor did not show unbounded generosity: Maria found herself cooped up in small, rather mean lodgings where, every evening, she would clean her only corsage. Many years later, the miserly Meneghini would nevertheless boast that he had showered jewels on his protégée,

Maria Callas during the famous recital at the Paris Opéra on 19 December 1958, wearing a breathtaking set of a diamond necklace and earrings, lent by the House of Van Cleef & Arpels.

who became his wife in 1949. Although he did give the singer her first jewels, he forgot rather too quickly that he bought them with the astronomical fees he demanded for arranging her performances. It was his habit, he later related, to give her a piece of jewellery at the opening night of each opera. Thus, he gave her a diamond suite for *Lucia di Lammermoor*, an emerald parure for *La Traviata*, and a ruby and diamond one for *Medea*.

The Medea suite, given to Callas in December 1953 after her triumph at La Scala, was bought at Faraone, a jeweller founded in Milan in 1860 that was frequented by important aristocratic Italian families and by Hollywood stars in the heyday of the Cinecittà studios in Rome. This set would remain one of the singer's favourites throughout her life. Although her luxurious jewellery was very well made, much of it did not come from the most famous jewellers – further proof, perhaps, of her husband's stinginess? The provenance of a necklace of emeralds and diamonds made up of twenty-four pear-shaped stones and of a ring set with a cushion-cut emerald of 37.56 carats would never be revealed, for example. It was easier to identify the origin of the branded jewels, for example those made by Harry Winston and acquired by Meneghini in 1957: a marquise diamond of 11.71 carats set in a ring, and diamond ear clips.

When it came to the soaring fees she commanded for her performances, Callas paradoxically claimed that money did not interest her, but that she needed to be paid more than anyone else. It is an admission that says a lot about her desire to be the first and the greatest – a desire fired by the competitiveness instilled in her by her abusive mother. Callas wrote to her husband that she wanted the best in everything, and most of all in her art. Hers was a voice that carried – and it carried a price. No other opera singer would be wealthier than she. It was a kind of revenge against the poverty and humiliation she had endured in her youth. She displayed the tawdry taste of the nouveaux riches: her apartment on the Via Buonarroti in Verona was bursting with kitsch objects, pink wall hangings and showy gilding – not unlike the stage scenery she had always known. What was beautiful must also glitter, she believed. Her jewels were not a mere fashion accessory – they proclaimed her wealth and success. They must be heavy, grandiose, like those of a queen who, in wearing them, imposes her power. She was superstitious, so also saw them as good luck charms.

AN ASTONISHING PHYSICAL TRANSFORMATION

Initially, Maria Callas paid little attention to her appearance – she was devoted above all to her art, not caring much for success or fame. Until the age of thirty she lived only through her voice, and the discipline it demanded. The year 1954, however, marked a turning point in how she and others perceived her looks and her femininity. Now honoured all over the world, idolized, famous and extremely wealthy, she decided to gild her triumph by bringing back to life a body she had for so long ignored. What good were the jewels she was given by her spouse if they went to adorn a thick neck or swollen fingers? What good was so much glory if she was not capable of mastering her own body? Her weight of 92kg (203lb) was her last weakness, the final battle that she must win over herself. It would take a little more than two years for her to weigh no more than 60kg (132lb). The nature of the diet she followed was the subject of endless fascination, with some people asserting that they had it on good authority she had ingested a tapeworm, while others claimed she had resorted to revolutionary new slimming programmes from the United States.

Callas was no longer an opera singer but a diva, a star like the movie stars featured in glossy magazines, like Audrey Hepburn whose elegance she envied and sometimes copied. La Divina, as Callas was known, now inspired the greatest couturiers in Paris and Rome, magazines dissected her divine wardrobe in minute detail and, in front of the camera, she displayed her precious jewellery as a little girl might her dolls. By the time she opened the season at La Scala, under the direction of Luchino Visconti, in December 1954, she had come to understand the power of a pared-down style and sober elegance. In her portraits she wore sensible strands of pearls, symbols of nobility and purity. Beautiful at last, and now the queen of La Scala, Callas aroused interest wherever she want. For some her voice was imperfect and graceless; others saw in it a dramatic power that went beyond mere technique to attain art and

Maria Callas, at home in Milan in the 1950s, proudly displays her treasures during a photo session organized by an Italian magazine.

supreme genius. In the Italian newspaper *Corriere della Sera*, the music critic Franco Abbiati praised the 'phosphorescent beauty' of her tones and 'her technical agility, which is more than rare – it is unique'.[13]

THE EXTRAVAGANT LOVE OF THE WORLD'S RICHEST MAN

But what would femininity and beauty be without love? Maria Callas's much older, miserly husband was no longer equal to her desire. For months, the Greek shipping magnate Aristotle Onassis had been trailing her, in Venice and in London, where he had had the façade of the Dorchester Hotel covered in red roses in her honour. As the two most famous Greeks in the world, their love seemed natural, inevitable; crowned with glory, she was the trophy that was still missing from the shipowner's triumphs.

A cruise on board the Onassis yacht in July 1959 destroyed all the thirty-five-year-old singer's certainties. It was both a floating palace and a tender trap that was closing around her. Onassis possessed the panache and sense of humour Meneghini had never had, and she allowed herself to be conquered. Callas did not open a single one of the scores she had planned to work on; all that she cared about was to live, dance and fall in love. Now at the centre of the jet set, she was like Violetta in *La Traviata* – drunk on her life of parties and amusements, to the point of losing her reason.

The divorce from Meneghini in 1959 was brutal – Callas lost part of her fortune. However, she retained her jewellery collection, her war chest. She was now a woman of her age and time, whom a super-rich lover – now also divorced – covered with gold and precious stones. It was rumoured that Onassis slipped gems into sorbets, matching the colours – strawberry for rubies, pistachio for emeralds … He was a regular at Van Cleef & Arpels, purchasing a diamond necklace, brooches, rings and an exceptional jewel of coral cabochons set with diamonds, pearls and turquoises. 'Ari's total understanding of women comes out of a Van Cleef & Arpels catalogue,' Maria was reported as saying. In 1967, from the same jeweller, she treated herself to a Cinq Feuilles (Five-leaf) clip, a platinum brooch set with diamonds and six Burmese rubies – her favourites.

A Five-leaf clip in platinum, rubies and diamonds, designed by Van Cleef & Arpels in 1967. Maria Callas would wear it, memorably, on a red voile dress at her last Paris concert in December 1973, at the Théâtre des Champs-Élysées.

The prima donna at home in Milan, wearing a set of rubies and diamonds by Farone, 18 October 1958.

HER BELOVED JEWELS, VICTIMS OF A FINAL BETRAYAL

On 20 October 1968, Maria Callas learned from television that her adored 'Ari' had just married that most famous of widows, Jackie Kennedy. It was a catastrophe from which Callas would never recover. Having distanced herself from her art for the love of this man, now she was left reeling. Her voice left her, even if her glory remained intact. In 1973, Callas embarked on a final swansong tour with the tenor Giuseppe di Stefano: seven months, eight countries, from Hamburg to Tokyo by way of Paris, Seoul and San Francisco. At the Théâtre des Champs-Élysées in Paris, she draped herself in purple veils and wore ruby pendant earrings and her matching floral motif brooch. In Japan, for the last concert she ever gave, Callas wore a strand of large pearls and matching teardrop earrings, which she had bought in 1971 at Van Cleef & Arpels.

She then returned to her lonely Parisian apartment, with its marble, gold and Louis XV furniture, and a palatial bathroom so vast and luxurious that she would sometimes withdraw there and even receive the few close friends she still permitted to visit her. The death of Aristotle Onassis, whom she had never stopped loving, on 15 March 1975 plunged Callas into mourning. The diva shut herself away from the world. All her sparkling jewels were returned to their casket, and only rarely did she wear a few sautoirs over black polo necks. Her hair was always pulled back into a ponytail and, having spent her life hiding her short-sightedness, she now wore heavy-framed glasses with thick lenses. This self-neglect and self-diminishment would lead her gently to her death, at the age of only fifty-three, on 16 September 1977.

Although Callas had long severed all contact with Meneghini, her fabulous jewellery collection went to her first husband because she died intestate. He himself died, childless, four years later. The jewels were supposedly passed on to those close to him – his nurse and a Greek pianist, it is said. And so, in November 2004, eleven flagship pieces from this collection appeared at auction. The owner, or owners, never revealed their identity, and the sale attained the astronomical sum of €2.19 million. None of Callas's jewels have been seen since.

Rose clip brooch, shown open and closed, Cartier, 1972. Yellow gold, rose gold, platinum, diamonds, emeralds, sapphires and rubies.

Clip brooch depicting a panther, Cartier, 1971. Yellow gold, emeralds, white chalcedony and lacquer. Maria Callas owned a brooch identical to this model.

Maria Callas in all her glory, wearing six strands of fine pearls, photographed by Cecil Beaton in 1957.

Ten pieces from the singer's jewellery collection on public display in Lugano, Switzerland, in 2004, before being offered for sale by auction.

'The world over, hanging from the walls of the long dusty tunnels backstage, your trains, your coats, your furs, your cloaks trimmed with ermine, your togas, your peplums, your stoles, your veils, your crinolines, your bustles – these are your garments of light! Piled up in wicker baskets from triumphant tours, your shawls, your lace, your tulles, your mantillas, your wigs, your caps, your fans, your gloves, your jewels, your pins, your fastenings, your crowns, your diadems, your tiaras, your laurels, Tosca's dagger – this too is You!'

YVES SAINT LAURENT

Fabulous stage jewellery

In 2003, an exhibition in Verona showed the many pieces of jewellery worn by Callas in the operas that won her her fame. They included the pearls she wore for *La Gioconda*, those for *I Puritani*, the ruby-coloured crystal jewels for *La Traviata*, the diadems for *Norma*, *Macbeth* and *Nabucco*, and the faux diamonds for *Tosca* – sublime fake jewellery conceived and made by the famous Marangoni workshop, founded in Milan in 1940 by Ennio Marino Marangoni and bought in 1990 by Swarovski, historically its crystal supplier. Marangoni also worked for Marilyn Monroe, Audrey Hepburn and, more recently, Madonna, Nicole Kidman and Elton John. The Marangoni workshop created pieces for Callas from 1947 to 1960, with the singer playing a highly active part in their design, often suggesting modifications. It was one of the ways in which she inhabited her roles. Like her clothing, the jewels were part of the character she was playing on stage, but they also needed to be light to wear and easy to put on and take off when changing costumes. 'It matters little that the jewels are "faux". They must above all be spectacular and, from a distance, give an idea of opulence while catching the light,' explained Delphine Pinasa, director of the Centre national du costume de scène (CNCS; France's national stage costume centre) in Moulins. 'Diadems, necklaces and earrings here have the function of forming a halo around the face, the better to make the character radiate. It is a tradition that goes back to the origins of the theatre and opera, when the stage was lit simply by candlelight: make-up and gleaming jewellery then made it possible to trace an outline in the dim light.'

Maria Callas in rehearsals for *Tosca* at the Paris Opéra, 18 February 1965.

AN EXCEPTIONAL COLLECTION OF 1960s JEWELLERY

Ava Gardner

In the 1950s, Ava Gardner – a farmer's daughter from North Carolina – was often said to be 'the world's most beautiful woman'. Her fairy-tale rise to fame would ultimately remain unfulfilled, but she assembled a superlatively elegant collection of contemporary jewellery.

In 1989, the announcement of the sale of part of Ava Gardner's jewellery collection was met with surprise, signalling as it did a downturn in the fortunes of a film star whose reputation had gradually become tarnished, with more than a whiff of *Sunset Boulevard* about it. Gardner's collection comprised mostly creations from her heyday in the 1950s and 1960s – timeless pieces of jewellery that were as glamorous as they were elegant, worthy of Hollywood's Golden Age.

EMERALD EYES

Ava Gardner was beauty personified. She liked to wear bright colours that mirrored her fiery temperament; her complexion was porcelain, her hair ebony, and her eyes a head-turning shade of iridescent green. She chose many of her jewels to match them – emeralds, jade and jadeite – but what came closest to reproducing her incandescent gaze were her 'flower' diamond earrings with interchangeable pendants: teardrop diamonds, pear-shaped pearls, or emeralds set with diamonds – the last, naturally, her favourites. Unsurprising, too, is that the most fabulous treasure of her collection was a ring with an exceptional step-cut Colombian emerald of 7.43 carats framed by diamonds arranged like petals. The emerald was of an intense green and of an exceptional purity, and had been set in 1961 by Van Cleef & Arpels, the company from which the actor bought most of her jewels. Also green, and from the same jeweller, were jewels made from jade, including earrings and a ring. Also outstanding was a very elegant four-strand pearl bracelet whose clasp was set with jade cabochons, made for her by the Beverly Hills jeweller William Ruser (1908–1994).

THE JEWELS OF A FEMME FATALE

'I'm kinda sentimental about my jewels,' the actor said, perhaps because they were sparkling proof of how far she had come from her origins – the youngest of the seven children of penniless North Carolina farmers, born on Christmas Eve 1922.[14] She owed her career and good fortune to the husband of one of her sisters, who photographed her and placed her portrait in the shop window of his New York studio. On catching sight of it, a theatrical clerk stopped dead on the sidewalk and told Gardner's brother-in-law to get in touch with MGM immediately, which he did. After putting her through a rapid audition, the movie studios employed the young Ava, aged just seventeen. 'She can't talk. She can't act. She's terrific,' Louis B. Mayer, the MGM boss, quipped in a telegram to a talent scout, delighted they had unearthed such a raw gem.[15]

The young woman was asked to sign a hastily drawn-up seven-year contract for a meagre $50 a week. Her strong Southern accent excluded her from parts destined for glamorous leading ladies, but she had the guts to work tirelessly to conceal her background and acquire the required trappings of elegance. Her marriage, in January 1942, to the hugely popular young actor Mickey Rooney, and their divorce just sixteen months later, brought about her rapid rise to fame: the popular press seized on her and her beauty, and the public was hooked. The young divorcee's jewellery collection included an engagement ring Rooney did not ask her to return – a step-cut diamond of 6.35 carats that was later reset by Van Cleef & Arpels into a diamond flower ring.

Gregory Peck, Robert Mitchum and Clark Gable became her partners of choice on screen, but it was Frank Sinatra who stole her heart. Gardner was a rising star, while Sinatra was suffering a lull in his career. He was married; she was a home-wrecker. They were consumed by their love for one another. What ensued was a torrent of fights and reconciliations, insults and drunkenness. Sinatra later recalled of falling in love with her that it felt as though she had put something in his drink. At their wedding in 1951, Gardner wore a broad smile that perfectly matched a double strand of pearls and a pair of pearl-and-diamond earrings. Two years later, they divorced. Freed from her toxic romantic relationships and already fêted for *Pandora and the Flying Dutchman* (1951), Gardner reached the zenith of her fame with *The Snows of Kilimanjaro* (1952) and *Mogambo* (1953), and then in the made-to-measure role of the unforgettable Maria Vargas in *The Barefoot Contessa* (1954). The role was the perfect incarnation of Gardner's inability to embrace happiness.

Ava Gardner at the peak of her artistry and beauty, around 1959.

Ava Gardner in 1954, photographed by Sam Lévin.

Some of the jewels offered for sale by Sotheby's. A bracelet with four strands of pearls, its clasp adorned with diamonds and cabochon jade gems, created by Ruser in the 1960s. A jade and diamond bouquet brooch, a pair of jade and diamond drop pendants suitable for Bouquet earrings, as well as a Fleur clip and a ring by Van Cleef & Arpels.

Ring ordered from Van Cleef & Arpels by Ava Gardner, adorned with the 6.35 carat diamond which featured on the engagement ring given to her by Mickey Rooney. Also shown are two Van Cleef & Arpels bracelets and a set consisting of a ring and earrings in diamonds and cultured pearls by Ruser.

LOVE WRITTEN IN DIAMONDS

Ava Gardner did not expect her husbands or lovers – some of whom were extremely rich – to give her jewellery. On the contrary, she appears to have bought most of her jewels herself. Notable among these was a ring consisting of an impressive cushion-cut Kashmir sapphire of 8.75 carats framed by diamonds, but pearls also featured heavily in her collection – a guilty pleasure she shared with many of her contemporaries. Pearls lit up the face, evoked a certain classicism, could be worn at any time of the day or night, and went admirably with diamonds … and furs! Ava wore pearls every day – around her neck, on her ears, in a ring and on her wrists. By the standards of the time her approach to jewellery could also be imaginative, as when she wore a Tiffany brooch with four uppercase letters in diamonds spelling L.O.V.E. Another brooch, by Van Cleef & Arpels, portrayed a gold cherub wearing a crown of fine pearls while seated on a cloud of Mississippi pearls encrusted with small heart-shaped rubies, and was engraved with a personal inscription to the actress.

Weary of Hollywood and its demands, in 1955 the world's most beautiful woman settled in Madrid, where the Argentine dictator Juan Domingo Perón, then in exile, was a neighbour. The latter regularly complained of the late-night noise coming from Gardner's house, where she held turbulent and drink-sodden parties (her alcohol addiction, she claimed, arose out of her shyness, not from any enjoyment). After such magnificent films as *The Night of the Iguana* (1964) and *55 Days at Peking* (1963), she appeared in *Mayerling* (1968) as the ageing Empress Elisabeth of Austria (Sisi), alongside the youthful Catherine Deneuve as the mistress of the crown prince. The cruel contrast between the two women hammered home the message that Ava Gardner's time was up. In 1968, she stepped back from acting and went to live London. Nevertheless, financial difficulties forced her to accept a guest role on the American soap opera *Knots Landing*, a long-running if lacklustre spin-off of *Dallas*. Her voice was cracked from smoking, her health was frail and her jewels were pawned. She died, alone, on 25 January 1990 from pneumonia, aged just sixty-seven, the victim of Hollywood myth-making and of an existence from which happiness had long been banished – if it had ever been present. On her bedside table in the hospital where she died was just one photograph: of Frank Sinatra and her. Ol' Blue Eyes, on learning of her death, was said to have muttered over and over: 'I should have been there for her!' He died eight years later.

JEWELLERY AS ARMOUR

Helena Rubinstein

According to Helena Rubinstein, a pioneer of the beauty industry, jewellery was endowed with immense power. Her fabulous necklaces and rings, which she wore in abundance, gave her both joy and consolation.

Drawing herself up to her full stature of 1.47 metres (4ft 10in), the inventor of modern cosmetics adored impressive jewellery. She is seen here in 1958.

Helena Rubinstein owed her lifelong devouring passion for jewels to a childhood gift and the emotion she felt on receiving it. The gift, from her grandmother, was a modest necklace of cultured pearls, but pearls for her would become so synonymous with joy and affection that, once wealthy, she gave strings of them to her friends and employees. Their brilliance had immediately fascinated her, as had the story she was told about them: how vast quantities of oysters carpeted the ocean floors but that only a very few contained a pearl. It was via the ocean that this young Polish Jewish woman, the eldest of eight daughters, gained her freedom: in 1896, aged twenty-four, she left the Kraków Ghetto and the prospect of an arranged marriage for the unknown shores of Australia. In the meantime, she changed her name from Chaja to Helena.

The young woman's mother financed the voyage by selling one of her last pieces of jewellery, but she also packed, in her daughter's only trunk, a dozen pots of face cream concocted by a chemist relative – for Rubinstein senior, a beautiful complexion was a passport to anything, and she insisted that her daughter always carry a parasol to fend off the sun. Once settled in the rural town of Coleraine, Victoria, Helena worked as a factotum in her uncle's grocery shop. Perched on high heels, Helena strove to disguise her 1.47 metre (4ft 10in) height, while her porcelain complexion earned her some envious glances from local women. It was here that she found her opportunity: at the age of thirty she founded a beauty institute in Melbourne, out of which she soon sold a lanolin-based cream she had developed. The purchase price of Crème Valaze – its name from the Hungarian for 'God's gift' – was thirty times the cost of production, and with her first profits, she treated herself to some Australian pearls, which, she said, captured the colour of the sea and the sky like no other.

A WOMAN WITH JEWELS IS WORTH DOUBLE

Helena Rubinstein had wider ambitions and wanted to conquer Europe. She embarked on a long voyage, stopping off in Ceylon (now Sri Lanka) en route. There she fell in love with sapphires, emeralds and rubies polished in the Indian style, rather than faceted in the European style, and these she began to accumulate with the reckless, greedy joy of a child. In London in 1908, she founded a branch of her cosmetics enterprise, followed by another in Paris, and then, after moving to the United States on the outbreak of the First World War, yet another in New York City. From then on, her company only grew and grew.

Not content with wearing just one necklace, Rubinstein layered two or three on top of each other, and emphasized their bulky, highly coloured opulence with earrings that almost touched her shoulders. She combined jewels worth millions with knick-knacks and trinkets unearthed in junk shops. Atop her cloche hat was a gigantic ruby that twinkled like an electric lightbulb, and she wore enormous jewelled rings on her fingers. She owned piles of them, one with a cabochon ruby of 115 carats and 175 diamonds, another featuring a cushion-cut sapphire of 70 carats, another still with a yellow step-cut diamond of 50 carats.

Jewellery gave Rubinstein her inimitable look. At every opportunity she would wax lyrical on its aesthetic power – not only for herself but for every woman: 'If I had been large, statuesque woman, I would surely have chosen simple, delicate jewellery, but since I am short and prefer simple, even severe clothes, I find they need big coloured stones. My hairstyle too is simple, but I personalise it with necklaces and long earrings.'

In her eyes, these pieces of jewellery were not mere accessories but rather the alpha and omega of her attire, as she explained in a long manifesto found among her papers after her death, entitled *Why I Love Jewels*: 'How marvellous to see jewels on someone's skin! A few strands of pearls can highlight the most sallow skin. Earrings of the right colour and shape make the pupils shine, even give a face character. An original ring gives grace and beauty to the shape of a hand, and there is nothing more beautiful than a jewel in the hair to heighten a charming hairstyle. Jewels are a woman's best friend, not only because of their market value but because they can bring the right note to a woman's femininity and personality.'

A young Australian woman of Polish descent, out to conquer America.

THE THERAPEUTIC BENEFITS OF JEWELLERY

Beauty, which Helena Rubinstein swore resided in every person, was her complete obsession: 'I know only beauty, that which moves me, charms me, captivates me, and stands the test of time,' she declared, hand on heart. Beauty was an art and a vocation, a veritable quest for excellence. 'There are no ugly women, only lazy ones,' fulminated Madame, as she had come to be nicknamed (her friend Coco Chanel was content with being just Mademoiselle). In Paris and London, followed by North and South America, even Asia, Helena Rubinstein launched an aesthetic revolution, using marketing, packaging and mail order to demonstrate that beauty was a way for women to liberate themselves. Proudly dressed in a white coat, standing at a lab bench, but nonetheless bejewelled, she made beauty into a science, offering women foundations and creams for different types of skin, lipsticks (previously reserved for actors and sex workers), and the first mascaras.

Industrial empires were typically run by men, and faced with them, Helena Rubinstein fought like a lion; she wrote that in this merciless war her jewels were the armour which gave her the courage a woman needed to compete with the opposite sex. She even felt a certain excitement in wearing excessive amounts of jewellery: touching her jewels, weighing them in her hand, sensing their weight on her ears, her wrists or round her neck was, according to her, a great source of pleasure.

Madame's beloved treasures also acted as anaesthetics, or soothing balms, in the face of emotional pain – she called the pieces she treated herself to after each misdemeanour by her first husband, the adored but unfaithful Edward W. Titus, her 'quarrel jewels'. The first of these was a necklace of fine pearls, which she bought after her husband had spent too long talking to an attractive young woman. Her second husband, Prince Artchil Gourielli-Tchkonia, twenty-three years her junior, was subjected to her intense outbursts of anger in which jewellery sometimes played a symbolic role. In 1953, during a transatlantic crossing on board the *Queen Mary*, a row blew up and she tore off her huge diamond earrings, wrapped them feverishly in a tissue with which she had just

The high priestess of cosmetics spent hours admiring her treasures and arranging them in alphabetical order.

wiped her brow, and, as her anger rose, threw them overboard. A few million dollars lost at sea …

A born collector, Rubinstein was a devoted fan of African and Oceanic art as well as of modern art. Dalí and Picasso both painted her portrait, in which she appeared heavily bejewelled, while the walls of her homes were covered with works by Matisse, Braque, Miró, Modigliani, Maillol, Léger, Brancusi and Dufy. She was a faithful friend and generous patron. She had a taste for collecting all manner of fine things. In her wardrobes hung all the genius of Dior, Chanel, Schiaparelli and Lanvin. She had a pronounced taste for furs, which she had decided went beautifully with her diamonds. Her jewellery collection include historic pieces: an emerald necklace that had belonged to Catherine the Great; a sixteenth-century cross encrusted with diamonds and amethysts supposedly possessed by the soul of a Crusader; ancient jewels given to her by a maharajah after she had lightened his wives' complexions; a necklace of rubies, pink diamonds and oriental pearls dating from the Renaissance; a fifteenth-century brooch in the shape of a rose set with diamonds, and Grand Siècle shoe buckles made up of intertwined double strands of pearls.

Rubinstein's travels were worthy of the Queen of Sheba. At the head of an empire on which the sun never set, she traversed the world, accompanied by her trunks stuffed with treasures. It was not unusual for her to present a stunned customs official with the contents of her vanity case – 'my junk', as she called her unbelievable arsenal of rubies, pearls and diamonds, all jumbled up with her pots of cream and lipsticks. During one of her countless long journeys, as she paraded covered in a cascade of precious stones, she explained that she was wearing only her 'travel rubies', meaning that the real ones had stayed behind in her jewellery box at home. She had copies made of most precious jewels, referring to them as 'lame ducks'.

Encounters with her were always memorable. The couturier Hubert de Givenchy and the editor

Multicoloured pearls were Helena Rubinstein's great passion. This four-strand necklace includes the most remarkable specimens.

Seen here in London in May 1963, aged ninety, at a lunch held in her honour by her niece.

of French *Vogue*, Edmonde Charles-Roux, always remembered one meeting with this high priestess of fashion, when she was smothered in jewels like an idol. Having kept them waiting, she appeared, adorned with fabulous roses of cut garnet stones, imposing carnelian stones and moonstones round her neck, on her ears, and right down to the buckles of her violet satin shoes. 'You are the reincarnation of Empress Theodora!' cried Charles-Roux, in a flabbergasted reference to the consort of the Byzantine ruler Justinian I (and former courtesan). Helena simply replied that they were just a few old things.

A HIGHLY MODERN JEWEL COLLECTION

Although she was a passionate collector of old jewels, Rubinstein could also be very avant-garde in her tastes and was especially fond of the jewellery of the 1930s and 1940s. The most daring of her jewels is without doubt a starfish-shaped hand ornament in diamonds mounted on platinum, with an extravagant faceted oval sapphire of 85 carats at its centre. This jewel, which covered the entire back of the hand from the wrist to the fingers, had been made from a mock-up by Anna Semenoff, a Russian painter and sculptor whose heyday was in the 1930s. One of Madame's most famous jewels was a very modern necklace of four strands of ruby pearls, emeralds and chrysoprases, separated by diamond rondelles, with a clasp of a cabochon emerald and diamonds. Two other necklaces of highly geometric design, dating from the end of the Art Deco period, were equally admirable: one blue and yellow, in sapphires and diamonds, made up of three detachable clips on the front, and the other set with ten cabochon emeralds linked together by baguette diamonds. Rubinstein's jewellery collection was so vast that it filled some ten *cartonniers* (ornamental storage containers for paperwork, like early filing cabinets). Her closest associate, Sarah Fox, explained that the jewels were arranged in alphabetical order: D for diamond, E for emerald, and so forth.

Rubinstein died of an embolism on 1 April 1965, aged ninety-two. Two days earlier she was still walking around her factory on Long Island, New York. At the time, her empire comprised fourteen factories around the world employing 32,000 people. As stipulated in her will, her jewellery collection was put up for sale in New York that same year. Friends, associates and jewellers, as well as the merely curious, flocked to the auction room, but the sale was not the success that had been expected. Many of the three hundred jewels on offer were deemed unfashionable – they were too bulky, too ostentatious. However, some of those then underappreciated pieces occasionally resurface in auction houses today and now command the prices they deserve.

A modernist Mexican necklace in silver, designed by William Spratling in 1940 — a series of rays inspired by the halo of the Virgin Mary.

A diamond ring of unknown origin.

Helena Rubinstein in New York in April 1964, a year before her death at the age of ninety-two, wearing an extraordinary necklace of seven strands of fine pearls.

THE JEWELS OF A DOWNFALL

Soraya

Queen of Iran for just seven years, then condemned to wander in exile for the rest of her life, Soraya would have been in a desperate situation had not the Shah of Iran showered her with priceless jewels.

The second wife of the Shah of Iran, photographed in her home near Rome in 1964, wearing fabulous ruby and diamond ear pendants.

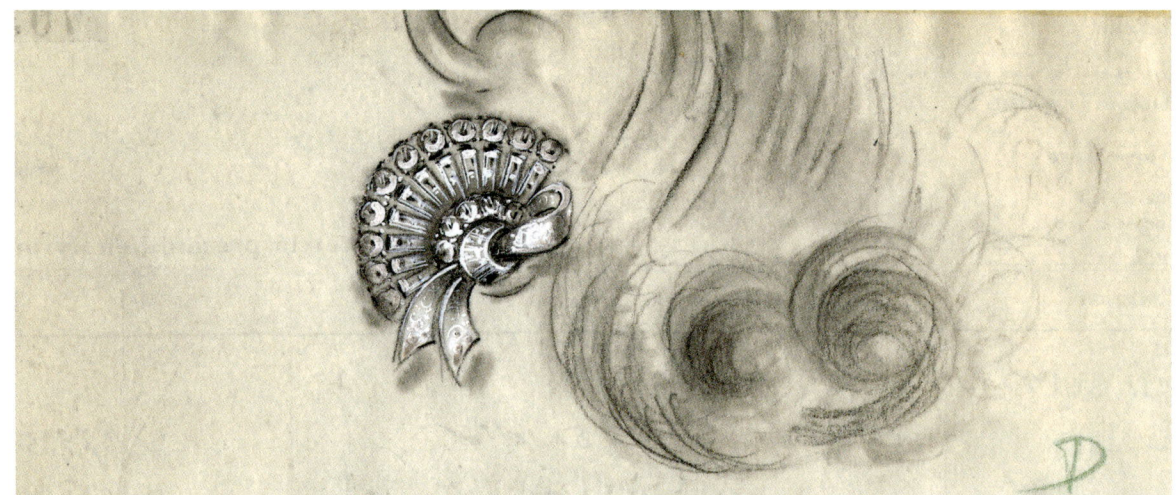

'Overwhelmed with premonitions, I have always had the foreknowledge, instinctively, of future events … In a way, I have been the victim of a strange destiny, contrary to my nature … My life will not have been entirely the one I would have wanted,' wrote Soraya in her memoirs.[16] Was it necessary that she endure great unhappiness for her to earn the nickname 'the princess with the sad eyes'? Yet everything had begun as if in a dream, in the arms of a man who, every morning, placed on her pillow armfuls of white roses and a jewel – most often creations by Van Cleef & Arpels, such as flower brooches, Mimosa clips or lovebirds in gold and diamonds. She had lived, for a time, inside a tale from *The Arabian Nights*.

IT WAS RAINING DIAMONDS

Born into a powerful Iranian family in 1932, Soraya Esfandiary-Bakhtiary grew up between Isfahan, Iran, and the great capitals of Europe. Her mother was German and she was educated at prestigious Swiss colleges. Soraya was stunningly beautiful and looked a little like Ava Gardner. In 1950, aged eighteen, she was living in London to perfect her English. Meanwhile, in Tehran, a search was under way among Iran's aristocratic families for the next wife of the shah, then aged thirty-one. Mohammad Reza Pahlavi's marriage to Princess Fawzia of Egypt, who had tired of her life in the Golestan Palace, had been dissolved under Egyptian law. A photograph of

Fan earrings made by Van Cleef & Arpels in 1950.
Empress Soraya adorned with diamonds from the crown jewels of Iran.

Soraya taken by a cousin of her father was shown to the shah, and he was swept away by her beauty and wanted to meet her immediately.

A very pleasant dinner was all it took for their official engagement to be announced the following day and a ring to be slipped onto the young woman's finger – an emerald-cut diamond of no less than 22.37 carats, far too big for such a small hand. What ensued was a love story in which the world's newspapers revelled. The wedding – postponed because Soraya had contracted typhoid – took place on 12 February 1951, and almost two thousand guests flocked to the palace. One and a half tonnes of orchids, tulips and carnations were flown in from the Netherlands, and Christian Dior himself made the journey to Tehran to present the bride with the dress he had designed: a creation onto which thousands of feathers, pearls and diamonds had been sewn. Despite such opulence, the shah had decreed that the ceremony would be modest, in view of the poverty then ravaging the country, and insisted that their wedding presents be replaced by donations to the poor. The Russian leader Joseph Stalin defied the order, giving the new queen a mink coat and a desk encrusted with black diamonds.

BULGARI, OR THE DELIGHTS OF ROME

In becoming queen, Soraya found herself in possession of a stunning jewellery collection including some of the world's most fabulous gems. From one official ceremony to the next, impressive parures of emeralds or diamonds enhanced Soraya's green eyes. In love and, in his words, 'happy as a child who had been given the moon', the shah spent lavishly at the great European jewellery houses. Reality struck home when, in the summer of 1953, he was involved in a failed army coup against the prime minister, Mohammad Mosaddegh, and the imperial

A clip depicting three birds, in platinum, yellow gold, rubies, sapphires, and diamonds, by Van Cleef & Arpels, 1954.

A clip depicting mimosa, in yellow gold and diamonds, by Van Cleef & Arpels, 1948.

Soraya Esfandiary-Bakhtiary, with the clip depicting three birds pinned to her lapel, married Mohammad Reza Pahlavi in 1951, before being repudiated in 1958 for having failed to produce an heir for him.

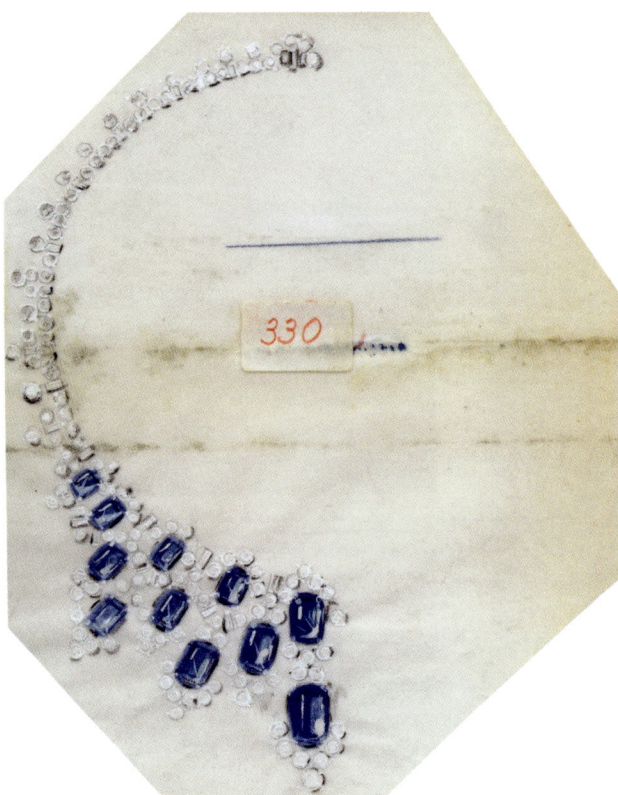

couple were forced into exile, though one spent in the luxury of the Hotel Excelsior in Rome. Soraya loved the Italian capital, and especially the Bulgari shop, to which her husband took her, doubtless in the hope of expunging the unpleasantness of their flight from Tehran. Among her orders were diamond and ruby earrings, a diamond necklace that included five sun motifs that could also be worn as brooches, and a sapphire and diamond necklace. A few days later, Mosaddegh was in turn ousted and the couple were invited to return to their marble palace.

Although Soraya was liked by a large proportion of the population and showed herself to be sincerely committed to her official engagements, she was nonetheless decried by religious conservatives, who considered her far too daring and Western. A photograph of her 'flaunting herself' in a bikini while waterskiing in Miami unleashed a scandal, to the point that the image was banned in Iran. The queen also had to endure the hostility of the shah's mother and sisters, including the formidable Ashraf, the shah's twin, nicknamed 'the Panther'. All of them fought fiercely for the shah's affections. But there was another cloud on the horizon – the queen's infertility. In October 1954, the shah's youngest brother was killed in an air crash, and the empire thus found itself without an heir: the fate of the crown now rested on Soraya's shoulders. Mohammad Reza was advised to take a second wife, something Soraya categorically rejected. This decision led, in 1958, to a divorce that neither of them wanted, but which was deemed to be in the country's best interests.

In Paris, 11 November 1991, at the gala 'The Best 1991'.

A preliminary sketch for a sapphire and diamond necklace by the House of Bulgari.

A diamond ring and a necklace in platinum and white gold by Bulgari, consisting of diamonds and twenty sapphires, the two largest weighing 15.3 and 8.16 carats.

REDEEMING JEWELS

Soraya's compensation for the end of her happy marriage came in the shape of a diplomatic passport, the title of imperial princess for life, a villa in Isfahan, an apartment in Paris, a generous monthly income and half a billion old French francs' worth of jewellery. Nothing, though, would erase the hurt, either for the shah or for Soraya, who was hounded by paparazzi and was referred to in the press as 'the princess with the sad eyes'. Her melancholy reputation was no doubt deepened by the succession of dramas that punctuated the rest of her life, with the men in her life so often meeting tragic deaths. Her greatest love, the Italian film director Franco Indovina, who tried to make an actor of her in the 1965 anthology film *The Three Faces*, died in a plane crash in 1972.

Following the Islamic Revolution, which toppled the shah in 1979, Soraya's income diminished. In 1988, a sale at Christie's of a few of her jewels – notably the teardrop pearl and diamond earrings given to her by the shah on their engagement, as well as a fabulous diamond necklace by Harry Winston, consisting of seventy-six navettes and thirty-eight pears – allowed Soraya to maintain her lifestyle. Having spent much of her life as a jet-set nomad, she ended up living in seclusion in her vast apartment at 46, avenue Montaigne, with its blue-themed decor of mosaics, Egyptian statuettes and Persian miniatures. She did not cope well with the passage of time and

At a premiere party in Paris, where the princess lived, 25 September 1986.
An impressive Bulgari diamond necklace, consisting of five detachable sun motifs, wearable as earrings and brooches.

sought solace in prayer, but soon neither make-up nor sparkling jewels could hide her languor and depression. Alcohol, cortisone and antidepressants were her refuge from anguish; she even feared she would be assassinated. Having cut herself off from everyone, she meticulously burned all her letters and photographs, as if she herself were fading away from the world. She died suddenly on 25 October 2001, aged just sixty-nine. Since no autopsy was requested, it was concluded that she had died of natural causes. Bijan, her younger brother, a faithful companion in her last years and her sole heir, arrived from Germany for the funeral, held in Paris. But a few hours before the funeral service, he too collapsed with a fatal heart attack. It was the final tragedy.

According to a will drawn up in 1991, in the event of Bijan's death, Soraya's fortune was to be divided between three French charities: the Red Cross, the Association des paralysés de France and the Société protectrice des animaux. Accordingly, in May 2002, a large auction was held at the Drouot-Montaigne auction house in Paris. The 942 lots fetched a total €6.5 million, two-thirds of which came from Soraya's vast jewellery collection. As well as her Harry Winston engagement ring, for which bids soared above €1 million, there were multiple Bulgari and Van Cleef & Arpels jewels, among them a diamond bracelet that concealed a watch dial. The jewels were all that remained of a love story.

A set of diamonds and cabochon rubies, as well a diamond and ruby ring by Van Cleef & Arpels.
The 'princess with the sad eyes' attends a party at the Institut Curie in Paris, 3 December 1986.

THE ART OF THE ACCESSORY

Jackie Kennedy Onassis

Refined and cultured but also materialistic, Jackie Kennedy Onassis was a woman full of contradictions. It was a combination that resulted in a jewellery collection that was as valuable as it was elegant – the collection of an icon.

The First Lady of the United States, photographed in 1960.

It is a photograph of infinite tenderness: a young boy in his mother's arms, playing with the strands of pearls around her neck; she is laughing, her head thrown back – Jackie Kennedy and her son John-John, in a picture that was seen all over the world. In 1996, two years after Jackie's death, the reappearance of this now iconic three-strand pearl necklace at an auction of five thousand of her treasures aroused much emotion. Until then, people had imagined it was an exquisite item made up of rare pearls, but the reality was quite different: they were fake, with an estimated value of just $500. On discovering this, the novelist Patricia Volk wrote of her disappointment in the *New York Times*: 'I want these pearls which will remind me, every time I wear them, of a time of potential, when I was seventeen years old, and a fairy tale seemed to be coming true, and I want history's pearls.'[17] She did not yet know that the whole world would fight over them.

THE POWER OF PEARLS

In the eyes of the world, Jackie Kennedy, thirty-fifth First Lady of the United States, made her mark as soon as she arrived in the White House as the true face of fashion. She was elegant and classic, while also being modern and inventive. Her clothes almost never varied: clean-lined tweed skirt suit or A-line

A private moment in the White House nursery in 1962. Jackie Kennedy, wearing her famous necklace of faux pearls, and her son JFK Jr.

dress with a pared-down cut, low heels, Hermès headscarf, Gucci bag (one of which even bore her name), oversized sunglasses and a pillbox hat perched on a perfectly sculpted helmet-like hairstyle – plus three strands of pearls, which she wore whether she was in official or informal dress. The pearls were already there when she got married in 1953, but rather than displaying them like a young lady of the smart set, a middle-class housewife or Queen Elizabeth II, Jackie endowed her pearls with a completely unexpected modernity. Pearls became her signature and so made their mark on history.

Decades later, during the 2024 US presidential election campaign, the Democratic candidate Kamala Harris likewise made her pearls a powerful symbol of her femininity. This was partly due to Harris belonging to the Alpha Kappa Alpha sorority, a historically Black women's university association with some illustrious members, such as the civil rights activist Rosa Parks, the writer Toni Morrison and the singer Ella Fitzgerald. On being initiated, each member receives a brooch with twenty pearls, a homage to the sorority's early leaders, a group of women known as 'The Twenty Pearls'. In 2024, a Facebook group, United by Pearls, was formed and called on its 500,000 members to wear pearls on the day of Kamala Harris's nomination – pearls worn with a raised fist.

Pearls were the First Lady's favourite accessory. These are fake — valued at only $500, they were snapped up for $211,500 at the auction held in April 1996.

TIFFANY & CO., OR NEW YORK ELEGANCE

Jackie Kennedy was a free woman. Freedom was written into her DNA and also into one of her school exercise books when she was just eleven: 'Ambition: not to be a housewife' – the phrase angrily underlined three times. Jackie would be a woman of the world, the most celebrated woman, the woman most on show – even if it meant using men to achieve her goals. 'I'm the guy who accompanied Jackie to Paris,' joked the president in 1961 on a state visit to France, during which his wife received particular acclaim. From adolescence on, Jackie aimed high. And it was a young senator destined for high office who caught her attention: a political animal, forceful and seductive. She was hoping for an intimate wedding, but a thousand guests – influential people, political supporters and many others – packed into their wedding garden party. On her finger was a beautiful engagement ring – a Toi et Moi by Van Cleef & Arpels, consisting of a superb emerald-cut diamond and a breathtaking emerald, while on her wrist was a bracelet loaded with twenty-five diamonds and eighteen pearls. For a man known to be extremely tight-fisted and always on the go, and who was already involved with other women, these were carefully chosen gifts. At that time, Jackie also acquired many jewels from Tiffany and Co., notably some brooches which she pinned to the lapels of her suit jackets. But there were also some very modern hinged bracelets by Jean Schlumberger, in gold and coloured enamel dotted with round closed-set diamonds, known as Croisillon bracelets, which Jackie owned in several colours. This item of jewellery, which is still available today, has since been renamed the 'Jackie' bracelet'.

Jackie's ambition to be free did not last long – she was too busy squandering her in-laws' fortune. Joe Kennedy, JFK's father, had made his fortune as a stock and commodity investor, involved in everything from Hollywood studios to Scotch whisky. Money flowed freely, and Jackie loved money

Some of the jewels belonging to Jackie Kennedy Onassis that were sold, at her children's request, by Sotheby's in New York in April 1996.
A 1985 advertisement for the Croisillon bracelets designed by Jean Schlumberger for Tiffany & Co. They were among Jackie's favourite jewels, and she owned them in several colours.

Colorplay

Jean Schlumberger's winning eighteen karat gold and enameled bracelets are available exclusively at Tiffany's.

Tiffany & Co.

DALLAS, GALLERIA · 13350 DALLAS PARKWAY · 75240 · (214) 458-2800 HOUSTON, THE GALLERIA · 5015 WESTHEIMER ROAD · 77056 · (713) 626-0220

passionately: it reassured her, and her punishing shopping sprees gave her relief. In January 1961, JFK reached the Oval Office, and Jackie followed in his footsteps, thinking of the fresh breezes she would soon send blowing through the dusty corridors of the White House – the French interior design company House of Jansen would restore this run-down dwelling to all its former splendour. On the eve of the inauguration, the couple strengthened their bond by sleeping in the same bed – apparently a not too frequent event. Two years and ten months later, she was seen crawling towards the rear of the presidential car, her raspberry-pink Chanel suit stained with the blood of her assassinated husband. Neither the Kennedy clan nor the American people were minded to give the presidential widow back her liberty, but it was not long before she was engaged in a new love affair with her brother-in-law Robert, a married man. He too was assassinated in Los Angeles in 1968. 'I despise America,' cried Jackie to Pierre Salinger, JFK's former press secretary, the day after Bobby's funeral, 'and I don't want my children to live here anymore. […] I want to get out of this country.' A man had been prowling around her for half a decade, ready to extricate her – the Greek-Argentine business magnate Aristotle Onassis.

A COURTESAN'S JEWELLERY COLLECTION

The world's richest man collected trophies, and Jackie was one of them, like Maria Callas before her. His manner was that of a peasant and he dressed like a mafioso, but he was attentive and generous. On board his yacht – a floating palace excessive in every sense – he poured diamonds at her feet and Jackie was able to smile again, while America was furious at losing its favourite widow. Before they were married, on 20 October 1968 – when he was sixty-five and she was thirty-nine – their prenuptial agreement passed through the hands of an army of lawyers: it contained 170 clauses stipulating, notably, the number of days she should spend with him and even the frequency of their physical intimacy. As part of the settlement, Onassis wrote her a cheque for 100 million francs, authorized her to shop as much as she liked and slipped onto her finger the famous Lesotho III – a fabulous diamond of 40.42 carats, marquise-cut from a stone of 601 carats that had been discovered a year earlier in the mines of Lesotho. The young bride, duly adorned, hastened to buy everything in sight from couturiers and jewellers, having the invoices sent to her other half before, it was said, returning her

Sitting in its case, the Van Cleef & Arpels engagement ring of diamonds and an emerald given by John Fitzgerald Kennedy to Jacqueline Bouvier in June 1953. Their wedding took place on 12 September of that year.

A set consisting of a ring and earrings, in rubies, diamonds and gold, by Van Cleef & Arpels, given to Jackie Kennedy by Aristotle Onassis in 1968, the year of their marriage. The pendants, featuring cabochon rubies, are removable. The ring is adorned with a heart-shaped cabochon ruby.

A stroke of genius: the Sunburst Brooch

In 1961, the Kennedys were invited to London for a state visit by Queen Elizabeth II. Jackie, with her sister Lee by her side, wandered the streets of the capital. At Wartski, the famous vintage jeweller, she was struck by a brooch called the Sunburst, shaped like a sun and set with diamonds. Not having the $100,000 required to buy it, she successfully offered the jeweller the diamond leaf brooches her parents-in-law had given her for her wedding in exchange. Shrewd diplomat that she was, Jackie was careful to order exact replicas of the jewels she had just exchanged so that she could appear to continue to wear them. The Sunburst only emerged for the first time a year later, in April 1962, during the visit to Washington by the Shah of Iran and the Empress Farah. Jackie was aware that the shahbanu would be richly bejewelled, while she possessed only a few modest trinkets. Dipping into her meagre jewellery case, she came upon the Sunburst and had the idea of attaching it to the front of her hairdo – in effect, a republican diadem. More radiant than ever, dressed in a powder-pink dress by Dior, Jackie caused a sensation. So much so that she wore the same outfit a month later, at a dinner with the French minister of culture, André Malraux. From then on, the Sunburst became one of the First Lady's signature jewels, pinned to her jackets or evening dresses. After the assassination of JFK, the Sunburst disappeared off the radar, as if it was somehow tied to Jackie's life in the White House. It reappeared only in 2009 and 2012, worn by her daughter, Caroline. It was one of the only jewels the latter had not offered for sale in 1996.

At a White House state dinner in honour of Grand Duchess Charlotte of Luxembourg on 30 April 1963, the First Lady wears her legendary faux pearls and, in her hair, her diamond sunburst brooch, bought in London.

purchases the next day to obtain cash. The cost was so exorbitant that the shipowner saddled his wife with the nickname 'Supertanker'. She also bought lavish houses, which she had decorated at great expense, supposedly inspiring Truman Capote to say that if given the Vatican, she would have the whole place repainted within forty-eight hours.

Soon, all Aristotle Onassis saw of his wife were the countless invoices she left in her wake. His death in March 1975 gave Jackie the opportunity to reprise her greatest role: that of widow. During seven years of marriage Jackie had had plenty of time to fill her jewel case, especially with pieces by Van Cleef & Arpels: two necklaces of rubies, emeralds and diamonds, with matching clip-on earrings and brooch; two Etruscan-style hammered-gold cuff bracelets; a ring with a large central ruby set with diamonds; emerald-and-diamond ear pendants; another pair with rubies and diamonds, and diamond clip-on earrings (Jackie did not have pierced ears, so wore exclusively clip-on earrings, which were very much in vogue during the 1960s and 1970s). She also loved the creations of two great Greek jewellers, Lalaounis and Zolotas – singular jewels in ancient or oriental style, which she wore notably in her summers spent on Onassis's private island, Skorpios. From this second bereavement until her death in 1994, 'Jackie O', as she was now nicknamed, led a discreet lifestyle, and on her rare appearances in public often did not wear any jewellery at all, in spite of having made a new life with a rich diamond merchant, a man who knew how to love her and also multiply her fortune tenfold. Even though she soothed herself with art and literature, money was forever in the foreground of Jackie's life – an illusory bandage to cover the insecurity that never left her, ever since the distant time of her parents' financial problems and divorce. Jackie died of lymphoma on 19 May 1994; she was only sixty-four, yet already there was something eternal about her.

A flower brooch in sapphires and diamonds.

Gérard Darel's black pearls

In May 1961, John Fitzgerald Kennedy and his wife Jackie were welcomed in Paris by General de Gaulle, and duly celebrated by the French people, who fell in love with this young woman whose maiden name was Bouvier — she had French ancestry via her father. She was perfectly elegant in her little 1960s suit, its simplicity highlighted by a modest necklace of black glass pearls. This jewel was then forgotten, only to gain fame again thirty-five years later. Danièle Darel, wife of the French king of prêt-à-porter, Gérard Darel, had always adored the elegance of Jackie Kennedy, so she jumped on the first plane to attend the auction of the former First Lady's possessions, held in New York on 23 April 1996. With her own money she bought, for the then colossal sum of $101,500, the black pearl necklace — almost worthless as an object, it was made desirable because of its link to the presidential couple's visit to Paris. On returning to France, the Darels quickly decided to bring the piece back into production. It went on sale for less than €200 and was a huge hit worldwide. It was available with one or two strands as well as in several colours, and was seen round the neck of such personalities as Susan Sarandon, Julia Roberts, Meryl Streep, Charlize Theron and Hillary Clinton. Today, Darel's Jackie Necklace is a must-have in costume jewellery.

John and Jackie with their daughter Caroline in 1961. The First Lady is wearing the black pearls that were later acquired by the couturier Gérard Darel for $101,500.

A necklace with a low market value that became an iconic jewel, with millions sold all over the world in many colours under the Gérard Darel label.

THE QUEEN OF JEWELS

Elizabeth II

It is impossible to think of Queen Elizabeth II without her jewels, from discreet strands of pearls by day to glittering diamond parures in the evening. Whether its value was sentimental, priceless or diplomatic, Her Majesty's jewellery spoke a language all of its own.

Her Majesty wears an imposing set of ruby jewellery on a state visit to Berlin, 24 June 2015. Created in the late nineteenth century for Queen Victoria, the necklace was originally set with diamonds and opals. Queen Alexandra, Victoria's daughter-in-law, had the opals replaced with rubies. Elizabeth II is also wearing the Girls of of Great Britain and Ireland diamond tiara she inherited from her grandmother, Queen Mary, who had been given it on her marriage in 1893. This piece was set with pearls before the Queen Mother had them replaced with diamonds.

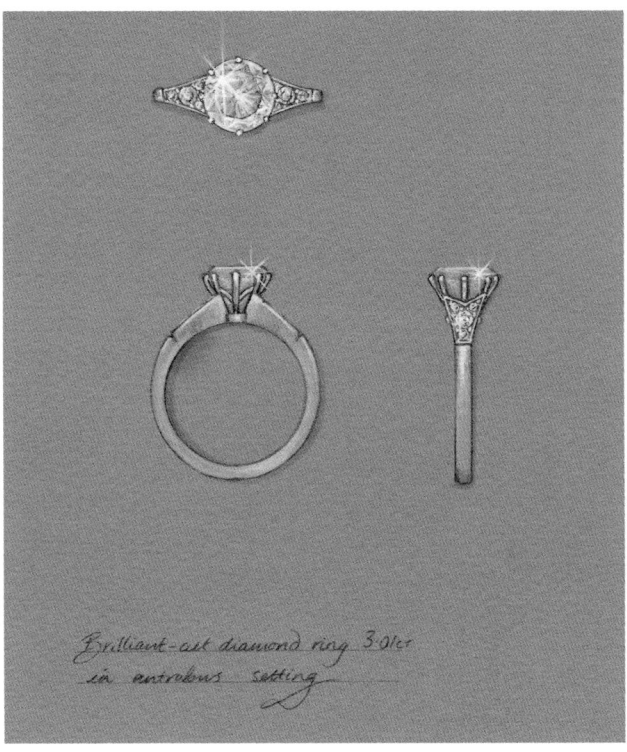

No woman was ever more richly bejewelled than Elizabeth II, Queen of the United Kingdom and other Commonwealth realms. So much so that, since her death at the age of ninety-four on 8 September 2022, royal commentators have scrutinized each appearance by Queen Camilla, Princess Catherine or Anne, Princess Royal, in the hope they might be wearing the late queen's treasures. Since Queen Victoria, the sovereign's personal jewellery has been separate from the Crown Jewels, which are the property of the nation. About three hundred pieces make up the queen's private collection, estimated to be worth €50 million and held in a family trust. A fabulous treasure, kept in strongrooms in the basement of Buckingham Palace that replaced a Second World War air-raid shelter. It is often believed that these jewels have been handed down over the centuries from king to queen, but in fact the oldest ones date back only to the nineteenth century, and most to the twentieth. Queen Victoria, inheriting a decidedly meagre jewellery collection, was the first to expand it, thanks, above all, to the help of the British jeweller Garrard, which created exceptional pieces with fabulous gems sourced from all over the British Empire – especially coloured gemstones from India and diamonds from South Africa.

SIMPLE BUT SIGNIFICANT RINGS

In her final wishes, the queen asked to be laid to rest wearing only a pair of pearl earrings and her wedding ring, which Prince Philip slipped onto her left ring finger on 20 November 1947 and which would never leave it. It was a simple ring, fashioned from yellow gold from the Clogau St David's mine in Wales and engraved with an intimate message that has always remained a secret. According to the queen's governess Marion Crawford, the love story between Philip and Elizabeth was one of the most sincere and profound in high society and began quite early. Crawford describes how, on a summer's day in 1939, as a young princess aged thirteen accompanying her parents on a visit to the Britannia Royal Naval College in Dartmouth, Devon, Elizabeth was unable to take her eyes off the officer cadet Philip Mountbatten. The young girl had already decided that she would love him, and no other. And so it was, until his death on 9 April 2021, two months before his hundredth birthday.

The first public appearance as a couple of Princess Elizabeth and Lieutenant Philip Mountbatten, 10 July 1947. On the future queen's finger is an engagement ring adorned with three diamonds from a tiara belonging to Princess Alice of Battenberg, Philip's mother.

The young queen wears the diamond necklace given to her on her wedding day by the Nizam of Hyderabad, then the world's richest man. Elizabeth II is believed to have subsequently given this jewel to Catherine Middleton on her marriage to Prince William in April 2011.

On 10 July 1947, the day her engagement was announced and four months before her wedding, the young princess, aged twenty-one, received from Philip a ring that she would wear next to her wedding ring all her life: a simple 3-carat solitaire set in a platinum mount, surrounded by ten small diamonds. Although these gems were light in carats, their significance was weighty. Indeed, on their engagement, the prince – Greek by birth, German by descent – was still impoverished, his only fortune residing in a diamond tiara passed on by his mother, Princess Alice of Battenberg, a great-granddaughter of Queen Victoria who had renounced her titles to take holy orders and even founded her own convent in Greece. This tiara was a historic jewel, for it had been given to her on her marriage in 1903 by the last sovereign of Russia, Nicholas II, and the tsarina, Alexandra. In 1947, Philip entrusted it to a London jeweller so it could be dismantled and the gems then used to create the engagement ring for Elizabeth, as well as a diamond bracelet given on their wedding day. The latter was a piece of which the queen was especially fond, and which she would lend, years later, to Princess Catherine – a sign of her affection for her grandson William's young wife.

The engagement ring, while modest compared to the thousand and one jewels belonging to the Windsors, remained the queen's favourite and even functioned as a kind of social weapon: whenever Her Majesty tired of a visitor, she had only to twist the ring on her finger for her staff to politely usher out the unwanted guest. As per the queen's instructions, this ring of incalculable sentimental value was passed on to her only daughter, Anne, Princess Royal.

Five years later, in 1952, for their wedding anniversary, Philip again gave his wife a highly symbolic jewel: another magnificent bracelet. In the meantime, the princess had become queen, and Charles

The Williamson brooch in platinum and diamonds, with the exceptional Williamson pink diamond, weighing 23.60 carats, in its centre. It was made by Cartier in 1953.

Here the Queen wears a set of sapphire and diamond jewels by Carrington & Co., a wedding present from her father, King George V, in 1947. The tiara was commissioned in 1963 from the London jeweller Garrard by the queen herself. Its gems were part of a jewel that Princess Louise of Belgium, crippled with debts, had been forced to sell. Also visible is the True Lover's Knot brooch, inherited from Queen Mary, who had herself bought it in 1912.

and Anne had been born. In order to take on the position of prince consort, Philip had to relinquish his career in the Royal Navy and even his Mountbatten name – and become a Windsor. The gold bracelet, designed by Boucheron, featured the prince's naval emblem set with diamonds and flanked by two sapphire crosses – doubtless a reference to the Greek flag. Another cross, of rubies this time, was framed by a pair of York roses, in reference to the queen's first title of Princess of York. The interlocking initials *E* and *P* of their first names featured on the scrolling link sections. Despite its sentimental value, the queen would wear this piece only rarely. In 1966, the prince added a new brooch to his wife's collection: Andrew Grima's Venus model, set with rubies and diamonds. It was a jewel she would wear on her coat towards the end of her life, on 22 May 2021, on one of her first official appearances after her husband's death – doubtless as a discreet act of homage and a token of love.

The queen wearing the Brazilian Aquamarine Parure in 1975. This necklace and earrings were given to her by the president of Brazil.

A YOUNG BRIDE'S TROUSSEAU

Elizabeth's wedding was an opportunity for her to considerably expand her collection of jewellery. Showing more of a penchant for corgis and thoroughbreds than for fripperies and jewels, before her wedding the young woman owned only two pearl necklaces and a few bracelets and brooches – including the Diamond Spray Brooch, given by the Royal Household staff for her twenty-first birthday; the City of London Lily Brooch, a gift when she received the Freedom of the City of London; and a pair of aquamarine-and-diamond double clip brooches, given by her parents on her eighteenth birthday, 21 April 1944. This jewel had been commissioned ten years earlier from the House of Boucheron by her uncle the Duke of Kent, who died, aged forty, in 1942. This piece of jewellery has gone down in history because the Queen is shown wearing it in her last official photographic portrait, in May 2022, which was revealed to the public only on the eve of her funeral, 18 September 2022.

On the occasion of Elizabeth's wedding – which brought her 2,583 presents – her parents, King George VI and Queen Elizabeth, made a suitably regal contribution to the trousseau, including a necklace of rubies and diamonds and a pair of diamond earrings that the then queen (later Queen Elizabeth The Queen Mother) had inherited five years earlier from Mrs Margaret Greville, a friend of the royal family. In 2002, Elizabeth II, in turn, inherited the entire contents of the magnificent Greville collection, of which many pieces came from the House of Boucheron as well as some jewels from the queen mother's personal collection. King George VI was no less generous, for he gave his beloved daughter an impressive piece of sapphire and diamond jewellery specially designed for her. Elizabeth later had the necklace shortened and a central cabochon added to it. Three years after the wedding, in 1950, the king also had made for his daughter an exceptional three-strand necklace comprising 150 diamonds.

The young princess could also count on the generosity of her grandmother, Queen Mary, who was a great lover of jewellery. From her own casket, the most lavishly furnished in Europe – she herself had received eighty-eight jewels on her wedding day – Queen Mary extracted handfuls of jewels: Indian bracelets, a fabulous bodice ornament encrusted with diamonds, 22cm (8½in) long, a diamond brooch in the shape of a knot, a pair of pearl-and-diamond earrings, a ruby-and-diamond bracelet, and a diamond tiara in neo-Gothic style known as the Girls of Great Britain and Ireland Tiara, certainly the one Elizabeth II wore most often during her reign. When, six years later, on 24 March 1953, a little more than two months before Elizabeth's coronation, Queen Mary died at the age of eighty-five, the new queen inherited the entirety of her legendary jewel collection. It included, notably, the diadem bought in the 1920s for the children of the Grand Duchess Maria Palovna, Grand Duchess Vladimir of Russia – a jewel worn in two versions, with pear-shaped pearls or pear-shaped emeralds – and eight diamond rivières which her grandmother liked to wear one on top of the other.

QUEEN VICTORIA'S FABULOUS TREASURES

Also in 1953, her coronation made Elizabeth the new owner of Queen Victoria's jewels, a collection handed down to each queen. It consisted essentially of diamonds, notably a choker made up of twenty-five very large diamonds, including a pear-shaped pendant, which Elizabeth wore on the day of her coronation and subsequently every year at the State Opening of Parliament. The pendant in question, and the earrings worn on the same occasion, were made up of three pear-shaped diamonds obtained (that is to say, extorted) by the British from the maharajahs of Punjab. The earrings' two pendants had been taken from a bracelet that had at its centre the famous Koh-i-Noor – the 'Mountain of Light'. This prodigious gem of 105 carats would later, in 1911, be mounted on the crown of Queen Mary, then, in 1937 on that of the future Queen Mother on the occasion of the coronation of her husband, George VI. Since independence in 1947, India has ceaselessly demanded the return of the gem, and Elizabeth II's death revived the controversy to the point that, on the day of the coronation of Charles III, Camilla wore the crown without the disputed gem.

Victoria's jewellery collection also contained a piece made up of impressive rubies of which the

queen mother was especially fond, as well as the Diamond Diadem, a crown of diamonds and pearls created two centuries earlier for King George IV. This was an item of jewellery that became emblematic of Elizabeth II since she wore it in so many of her official portraits, including those reproduced on banknotes and stamps. It features national emblems: a rose for England, a thistle for Scotland and a shamrock for Northern Ireland.

The queen, motivated by a sense of duty and an awareness of posterity, in turn considerably enriched the collection she had inherited, particularly by acquiring historic pieces put up for sale by the biggest auction houses, such as a necklace of sapphires and diamonds from the Austrian branch of the House of Saxe-Coburg, one of whose princes, Albert, Victoria had married. Elizabeth had the necklace made into a diadem in order to wear it with the sapphire jewel her father gave her in 1947.

JEWELS AS OBJECTS OF DIPLOMACY

Her birthdays, marriage and coronation were occasions for magnificent gifts bestowed by friendly nations or member countries of the Commonwealth. The first, on her twenty-first birthday, was a diamond necklace given by the South African government after her visit to the Kimberley diamond mines, owned by De Beers. She wrote of its impressive beauty to her grandmother, Queen Mary, who she knew had a mad passion for diamonds. Mir Osman Ali Khan, the Nizam (ruler) of Hyderabad State and one of the world's richest men, gave her a diadem consisting of three floral motifs in diamonds and a Cartier diamond bracelet. The queen had the diadem dismantled in 1973 in order to make – along with diamonds and ninety-six rubies gifted by Burma – a tiara she would wear for the first time in Japan in

The necklace and earrings Queen Elizabeth II wore at her coronation, and Queen Mary's Dorset Bow brooch, on display at Buckingham Palace, 23 July 2015.

Her Majesty, wearing her coronation jewellery, at the official opening of parliament in Trinidad and Tobago, February 1966.

1975. In November 2023, this jewel diadem was worn by Queen Camilla at a state dinner for the president of South Korea, Yoon Suk-Yeol. As for the Nizam's necklace, Elizabeth appears to have given it to Catherine on her marriage to Prince William in April 2011, since the princess wore it, notably, in February 2014. Other diplomatic presents included some enormous aquamarines given by Brazil, which between 1953 and 1968 were made into a diadem, bracelet, brooch, earrings and necklace – their pale colour a perfect complement to the queen's eyes. There were numerous other smaller jewels, notably a pink diamond from a South African mine which, once cut, weighed 23.60 carats and became the centre of a flower-shaped brooch designed by Cartier. King Faisal of Saudi Arabia gave Her Majesty two Harry Winston diamond necklaces during his state visit in 1967, while the Emir of Qatar, Khalifa bin Hamad Al Thani, gifted a diamond swag necklace with a centrepiece of two red rubies on his state visit in 1985. The queen also received a splendid emerald and diamond necklace – formerly, it is said, in the collection of Empress Joséphine of France – from two elderly British sisters who had remained unmarried.

Despite the richness of her jewellery collection, undoubtedly the most fabulous in the entire history of jewellery making, we may wonder whether Queen Elizabeth II had a real taste for jewellery – whether her jewels were not merely emblems, which she considered more part of her official uniform than fashion accessories, inseparable from her role and from the image she felt duty-bound to present to the world. The British monarchy is the symbolic guarantor of the power of the state, and its queen is therefore required to maintain an absolute reserve and neutrality.

Nonetheless, since everything says *something*, this silent sovereign was able to express herself through her wardrobe and her jewels. Each jewel told a story, evoked a memory or paid homage. Every one of her brooches, numbering around one hundred in total, sent a discreet yet powerful message. Thus, on 9 April 2021, at the funeral of the man with whom she had shared seventy-three years of her life, Elizabeth II wore the Richmond Brooch, a love-jewel worn by her grandmother, Queen Mary, during her honeymoon at the start of the previous century. Another tender message was conveyed when, in her televised Christmas Day speech in 2002, nine months after the death of the queen mother, Elizabeth wore the Centenary Rose Brooch, a rock crystal cabochon set with a hundred diamonds, which she had given to her mother two years earlier, on her hundredth birthday.

The queen's jewels, like her clothes, could even convey political messages. There was much comment on the blue hat dotted with little yellow stars, seen as a reference to the European flag, which she wore to the State Opening of Parliament in 2017, the year after the referendum on the UK's future membership of the EU. In the course of her countless journeys, the queen always honoured her hosts through her choice of jewellery. On her first visit to Canada in 1951, and then again in 2017 for the celebrations of Canada's 150th anniversary, she wore a brooch in the shape of a maple leaf, which had been given to the Queen Mother in 1939. She would lend it to Camilla in 2009, and to Catherine in 2011 and 2016, for their own respective visits to Canada. Numerous brooches embodied her attachment to the Commonwealth, such as the New Zealand Silver Fern Brooch or the Australian Wattle brooch, the latter featuring Australian tea tree blossom and mimosa, in addition to golden wattle, Australia's national plant. Likewise, during her visit to the Republic of Ireland in 2011, the Queen was careful to wear the Girls of Great Britain and Ireland Tiara given by the people to her grandmother Queen Mary in 1893. This thoughtfulness attracted especial comment as Elizabeth II was the first British sovereign to have visited Ireland in a hundred years. In the same year, she received Abdullah Gül, the Turkish president, and was careful to wear, at dinner, a breathtaking brooch whose diamonds had been given to Queen Victoria by the Ottoman sultan, Abdülmecid I, in 1856. Through such nods to shared history and as a symbol of ongoing friendship, jewels place the wearer in a line of descent and inheritance which are the very foundations of monarchy. The queen was a beacon in the fog of history, and her jewels were like the shining white pebbles of Hansel and Gretel, leading people home through the dark and the gloom. Other queens and princesses had worn them before her, and others would wear them after her. The thread was not broken.

One of the queen's favourite diadems, the George IV State Diadem set with pearls and diamonds, was created in the early nineteenth century. It was one of the three crowns worn by the queen for ceremonies of state, most notably for the carriage ride from Buckingham Palace to Westminster for the opening of the British parliament. It was the custom that once in Parliament, she then wore the Imperial State Crown. In 2019 she broke with protocol, choosing to retain the George IV State Diadem, which is lighter.

Created in 1911 and initially adorned with the Koh-i-Noor diamond (105 carats) and the Cullinan III and IV diamonds, Queen Mary's crown has often been modified over time. It was worn by Queen Camilla at her coronation in February 2023 – without the Koh-i-Noor but featuring the Cullinan III, IV, and V diamonds, and lacking four of its eight half-arches.

102   Women and Their Jewels

The world's biggest diamond

It is impossible to examine the queen's jewellery without evoking the the Cullinan Diamond. In January 1905, in Transvaal Colony (part of Britain's South African territories), a stone as big as a man's fist came away from the rock in the Premier No. 2 mine, near Pretoria. The miner had just discovered the world's biggest diamond, weighing 621g (almost 22oz), or about 3,106 carats, which was immediately named after the mine's owner, Thomas Cullinan. As a mark of loyalty and gratitude, the stone was soon after offered by the government of Transvaal to King Edward VII. Work on cutting it began in Amsterdam — an operation that would take more than a year. Nine main stones and ninety-four smaller ones were extracted from it: the biggest, Cullinan I, weighing 530 carats and pear-shaped, was destined for the sceptre; the second biggest, Cullinan II, weighing 317 carats, for the imperial crown. Cullinan III was a pear-shaped stone of 94.4 carats, and IV a cushion of 63.60 carats. These two diamonds were offered personally to King George V, who was crowned in 1911. His wife, Queen Mary, first had them set in her crown, then made into a pendant and finally into a brooch. This brooch, which was worn subsequently by Elizabeth II, notably on the day of her Diamond Jubilee, has an estimated value of €14 million.

Queen Mary also made good use of the other 'smaller' Cullinan diamonds, with some being set into brooches or pendants. Notable among these was number VII, with a marquise cut, which became one of the two pendants on a necklace made of fabulous emeralds. This one was destined to bring Queen Mary out in a cold sweat, for her brother, Prince Francis of Teck, who died prematurely, had bequeathed the precious stones to one of his mistresses. Having finally retrieved them after some negotiations, the queen had an extravagant set made, featuring cabochon emeralds that looked a little like mint sweets, which she wore on the occasion of the Delhi Durbar in December 1911. These jewels were often worn by Queen Elizabeth II.

Queen Mary, grandmother of Elizabeth II, wears a brooch made up of the imposing Cullinan III and IV diamonds.

More than 3,000 stones for a crown

No fewer than 2,868 diamonds, 273 pearls, 17 sapphires, 11 emeralds and 5 rubies made up the Imperial State Crown for the coronation of George VI, Elizabeth II's father, in 1937. It was a replica of an earlier crown made in 1838 for Queen Victoria, but designed to be lighter — though it still weighed 910g (32oz). For the coronation of Elizabeth in 1953, the height of the crown was reduced by 2.5cm (1in). The queen would wear it to every State Opening of Parliament of her reign. It was rumoured that on those days, Her Majesty would breakfast and read the newspapers while wearing the crown, so that she could get used to its cumbersome weight. The stones of which it was made up were historic, especially the Stuart Sapphire at the back of the band — a stone of 104 carats dating back to 1214, one of the oldest known. At the front, taking centre stage, were the famous Black Prince Ruby, actually a spinel, and the Cullinan II. This crown was placed on the queen's coffin at her funeral in 2022.

The Imperial State Crown, created by the jeweller Garrard in 1838 on the occasion of Queen Victoria's coronation.
Elizabeth II at the State Opening of Parliament in 1987 in London.

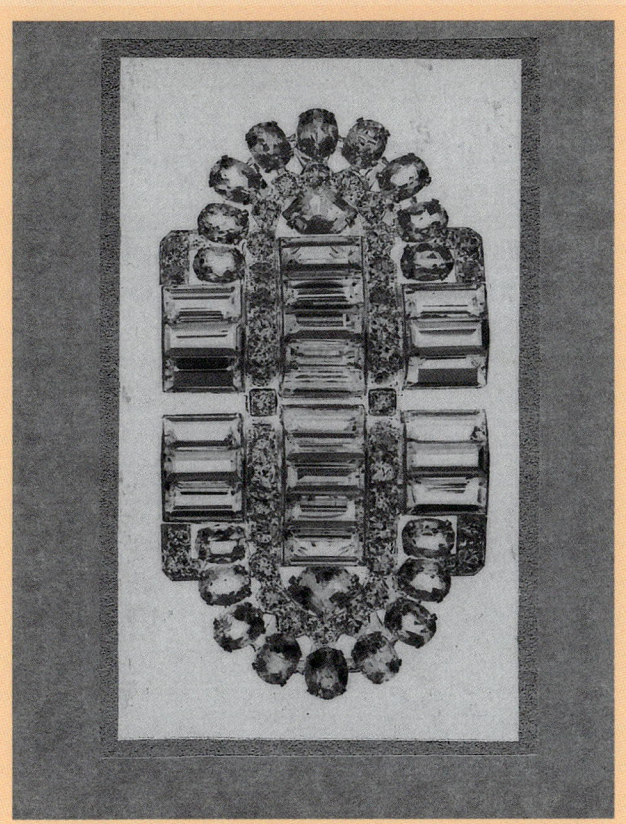

A taste for pearls

The queen showed little imagination in the way she wore jewellery — perhaps deliberately, always displaying an unchanging combination: formal dress enlivened with a diadem, earrings and a necklace of precious stones, with bracelets worn over white gloves. Other than her engagement ring and wedding ring she rarely wore rings, and always wore a sparkling brooch pinned to her upper left chest, on the side of the heart. There was, of course, the ever-present parure of pearls: earrings plus a necklace of one, two or three strands. The pearls were always natural pearls of the highest quality and were her signature, the main accessory of her outfits. Her ancestor Queen Victoria, devastated by the loss of her prince, had exchanged her ostentatious diamonds for her sets of pearls, which for the last four decades of her life symbolized the tears she would never stop shedding.

The most iconic of Elizabeth's many pearl necklaces was a three-strand model, worn with her brightly coloured suits or her pastel twinsets. It was an extremely precious item, valued today at £1.03 million ($1.38 million), but whose value for Elizabeth was above all sentimental, because it was given to her when she was a young girl by her father, King George VI. Her daughter, Princess Anne, who is passionate about pearls, inherited this necklace in September 2022. As for Catherine, Princess of Wales, she received another of the queen's pearl necklaces, a four-strand choker featuring an imposing central clasp set with diamonds. She wore it at the sovereign's funeral and the second coronation of King Charles III, in Scotland, in July 2023.

The Queen on a visit to Tuvalu, in Polynesia. She is wearing her perennial three strands of pearls, as well as the Cullinan V brooch.

On 31 July 1937 the Duke of Kent, Elizabeth's uncle, bought a double clip of aquamarine gems and diamonds from Boucheron. He died in 1942, and this jewel was then given to the future queen for her eighteenth birthday in 1944. She would wear it many times, notably in this final official portrait, in May 2022, shortly before her Platinum Jubilee.

AN OBSESSION WITH TIARAS

Barbara Hutton

Over the course of her seven marriages she was a princess, a baroness and a countess, with a panoply of jewellery befitting her rank. The woman whom America dubbed the 'Poor Little Rich Girl' found, in her collection of jewels, unhoped-for pride and comfort.

The Countess Kurt Haugwitz-Reventlow (who was born Barbara Hutton) in the 1930s, wearing diamond and moonstone jewellery by Van Cleef & Arpels.

When Barbara Hutton was little, her grandfather already called her 'Princess' – a name she also gave to her Shetland pony, regardless of the fact it was male. Servants had the choice between 'Princess' or 'Your Highness' when addressing their young mistress. It is hardly surprising, then, that she soon developed a love of tiaras and a mania for wearing them every day. For all that, there was nothing idyllic about this young girl's life. In 1917, at the age of five, she discovered the lifeless body of her mother, widely believed to have died by suicide to bring an end to her life of unalloyed misery. Since her father, Franklyn Hutton, was permanently absent, Barbara ended up in her grandparents' neo-Renaissance palace, one of whose fifty-six bedrooms, cluttered with Gothic furniture, she made her home. She was seven years old when the head of the clan, entrepreneur Frank Winfield Woolworth, died, and millions cascaded down to this child, whom her family agreed they would keep apart from the world, well away from potential fortune hunters. Forty years earlier, her grandfather had set up his first business, and since then some two thousand five-and-dime stores had sprung up all over the United States. The fortune was colossal, and Barbara was the richest little girl in America.

MARIE ANTOINETTE'S PEARLS

As a child, already feeling burdened by her fortune, Barbara Hutton asked her aunt whether she could get rid of it, but her millions, it seemed, would be her cross to bear. In her loneliness, the little girl distributed toys and jewellery among her friends so that they might deign to come back and play with her. It was a modus operandi which, all her life, she would never abandon. On the evening of her eighteenth birthday, an unforgettable party was thrown at the Ritz in New York, and the French singer Maurice Chevalier was paid handsomely to hand a diamond to every female guest. The young heiress simply begged to be loved, and she would never be short of courtiers or, for that matter, husbands – there were seven in all, each involving a magnificent wedding and cascades of jewellery. Blue blood was her weakness, so her first love was a self-styled Georgian prince, Alexis Mdivani, whom she married at the age of twenty-one in the St-Alexandre-Nevsky Russian Orthodox church in Paris. Handsome and possessing a wild and frivolous temperament, he was first and foremost a penniless fortune hunter. With the allowance from his recent divorce, he treated his golden goose to a fine ring, set with a black pearl. He also splashed out on an exceptional pearl necklace, although this was paid for with Barbara's money. On her wedding day, the young bride flaunted a diamond necklace and, most importantly, was crowned with a Balinese tortoise-shell-and-diamond tiara, ordered from Cartier on her return from a trip to Bali.

Not to be outdone, Barbara's father had acquired from Cartier a pearl necklace said to have once belonged to Marie Antoinette. Barbara could not have dreamed of anything grander. It was indeed an exceptional necklace, which its previous owners had had shortened or lengthened, according to fashion (it would subsequently reappear at a 1992 auction, when it comprised forty pearls). From then on, pearls became Barbara Hutton's great passion: she acquired another necklace with two strands of pearls and an opal-and-diamond clasp – attributed to Cartier – as well as a necklace of golden pearls, another of black pearls, and several more of jade pearls, including a fabulous one also given to her by her father on her first marriage, which sold for $27 million in 2014, or more than $1 million per pearl. Much as Franklyn Hutton was often absent from his daughter's life, he soon bore the cost of her great passion for jewels – as on one summer's day in 1929, while on a trip to France, he offered to buy her a ruby from Cartier, and the teenager, faced with the suggested choice of gems, chose the finest and most expensive, costing around $50,000 (some $1,150,000 or £850,000 in today's money).

A Cartier necklace commissioned for Barbara Hutton in 1934. Jadeite, platinum, yellow gold, diamonds and rubies (see also page 114).

A CASKET FILLED WITH HISTORIC JEWELS

Always in search of blue blood, craving aristocratic status, tiaras and palaces, America's 'Poor Little Rich Girl' collected men who were in a position to grant her dream of being a princess. It mattered little that they were impoverished: they had the titles, she had the money. 'The prince is dead. Long live the count,' sneered the press on the announcement of Hutton's divorce from Mdivani to make way for a her wedding with Count Kurt Haugwitz-Reventlow, who would become the father of her only child, a son. Her infatuation with Frederick of Prussia, a great-great-grandson of Queen Victoria, put an end to the marriage. She later went on to wed Prince Igor Troubetzkoy, who had jade-green eyes and the body of Adonis, and Baron Gottfried von Cramm, a superb tennis player who preferred the company of men.

She also tied the knot with a few commoners, though even they had pretensions to grandeur: Cary Grant was in the first rank of Hollywood stars, and Porfirio Rubirosa was the prince of gigolos, having already made conquests of Marilyn Monroe, Danielle Darrieux, Jayne Mansfield and Zsa Zsa Gabor (her marriage to Rubirosa lasted just fifty-three days). Hutton's last husband was a modest chemist named Raymond Doan, but she was able, at vast expense, to secure for him a title in Laos, as Prince Vinh Na Champassak – making her, of course, a princess.

Barbara Hutton never married without a jewellery case worthy of her latest title, and throughout her tumultuous life, she bought historic, even royal, pieces, including creations fit for a queen – an extravagant ruby and diamond necklace set made by Chaumet in 1897, for example, which she wore throughout the 1930s before having it converted into a tiara-necklace in the Egyptian Revival style by

Barbara Hutton, then Princess Mdivani, wearing her ruby necklace at the lavish birthday party given in her honour at the Ritz in Paris.

A sumptuous parure in rubies and diamonds created by Chaumet, photographed here in its case shortly before it was delivered in 1897. The whole set was completely re-mounted by Van Cleef & Arpels during the Second World War, turning it into a ruby necklace, known as the 'Papyrus necklace', often worn by the wealthy heiress.

Barbara Hutton, photographed by Pach Brothers Studio wearing her favourite necklace, consisting of twenty-seven beads of the purest jadeite dating from the eighteenth century, as well as the matching ring and bracelet on her right hand — three creations by Cartier.

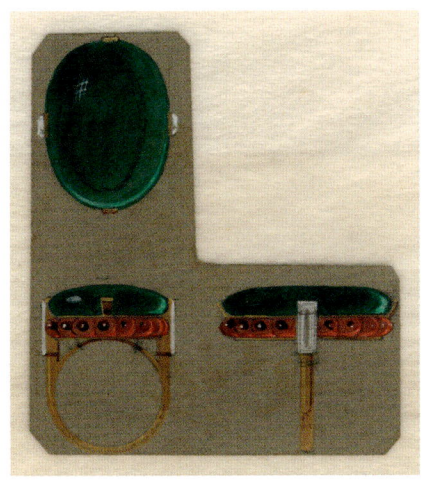

Van Cleef & Arpels in the early 1940s. This disappeared off the radar for half a century, before showing up again at an exhibition held by Van Cleef & Arpels in Geneva in November 2013. Fond as she was of royal treasures, at Bulgari the billionairess acquired 'the finest gem in the Egyptian Treasury', a fabulous 40-carat diamond that in the nineteenth century had belonged to the Egyptian general and politician Ibrahim Pasha, before King Farouk sold it to the Italian jeweller. Hutton had the gem recut so she could wear it on a ring, an imposing solitaire she would keep until the end of her life.

A MYSTICAL CONNECTION WITH HER JEWELS

Barbara Hutton was of a whimsical bent: she liked to give colours to days – Monday was mauve, Tuesday green, Wednesday red and so on – so naturally she wore clothes and jewellery to match. Her passion for jewels was sensual and obsessive: she would try them on and admire them in front of the mirror, and would go through them for hours, feeling their weight in her hands. These masterpieces of the jeweller's art represented for her the perfect harmony between nature and humanity. A jeweller was thus, in her eyes, a maker of dreams, to be subjected to her confidences for hours on end and then commissioned to fulfil her desires. Pierre Arpels was one such treasured witness: in 1967, he created for her a regal diadem whose central pear-shaped diamond weighed 54.12 carats, with a further six large pear-shaped diamonds. The jeweller was astonished when the following year she received him in her suite at the Ritz in Paris – unwell, confined to her bed and in her nightgown, but wearing her diamond diadem. During this unforgettable visit she placed an order for two Indian-style rigid bracelets in yellow gold, set with large pear-shaped diamonds, and matching earrings. A tireless traveller, and with a particular passion for Asian art, she often brought back gems and jewels from her many extended trips abroad and

Designs for a platinum, gold, jade, ruby and diamond ring by Cartier, 1934, as well as the completed ring. A gold, platinum, jade, ruby and diamond pendant earring by Cartier, 1934, and a platinum, jade, ruby and diamond bracelet by Cartier, 1933, made for Barbara Hutton.

Barbara Hutton, who was fascinated by big cats, bought several brooches and bracelets from Cartier: in 1957, a clip brooch depicting a tiger, in yellow gold, diamonds, emeralds and onyx, and in in 1962 a tiger bracelet in gold, jonquil diamonds, emeralds and onyx. Design for a tiger brooch, Cartier Paris, 1965, in yellow gold, emeralds, onyx and yellow diamonds. Barbara Hutton owned a similar piece.

Opposite: On the wedding day of her only son, Lance Reventlow, in 1964, she wore a double strand of pearls and a tiger brooch by Cartier.

subsequently had them fashioned into pieces that were hybrid in style.

Condemned to utter boredom and an impossible quest for happiness, Barbara Hutton was a queen in perpetual exile, always escaping from one continent to another. From 1946, she ruled over the medina in Tangier, where she had had an improbably luxurious palace built, before settling at the foot of a snow-capped volcano in Mexico. The volcano reminded her of Mount Fuji, so naturally she commissioned the building not of a hacienda but of a traditional Japanese house, which she even furnished with a kabuki theatre where artists from Japan performed. In her various palaces, Hutton struck the attitude of a queen, supremely comfortable with the outrageous accumulation of treasures that surrounded and adorned her. Kilos of pearls, rubies and diamonds festooned her neck, clustered at her wrists and were wedged onto her slender fingers. She detested moderation, she said.

DECKED OUT UNTIL HER LAST BREATH

As the years passed, Barbara Hutton's colossal fortune melted away. In terminal decline, she lingered on in a Los Angeles hotel, made up like a sad clown, her diadem awry and smothered in the jewels of her past glory – a victim of her washed-up dreams. She was frighteningly thin, her arms as gnarled as dead wood, mangled by injections of amphetamines and morphine. She was like a Venetian bridge that had never reached the other bank, she wrote with jaded wit. Around her neck, among her pearls and diamonds, she wore a whistle, used for making a battalion of nurses, a baroness secretary and a countess assistant stand to attention. She required them to wear gowns and little silver bells around their necks so she could hear them moving about. Her so-called right-hand man stole her belongings and sold off her works of art to the highest bidder. At her death, on 11 May 1979, in her sixty-seventh year, Hutton's bank account had a meagre balance of $4,000, though her fabulous collection of jewellery had in part been preserved. Her butler pulled the Pasha diamond off his dead mistress's finger and put it in a supermarket bag, along with the contents of three jewellery caskets, and the whole was deposited in a bank in Bermuda. There followed a fairly mysterious sequence of events, at the end of which, from 1985 onwards, treasures that had once belonged to the Poor Little Rich Girl occasionally turned up at auction.

Designs for a pair of ear pendants in diamonds and pear-shaped imperial jade gems, Boucheron, 1930.

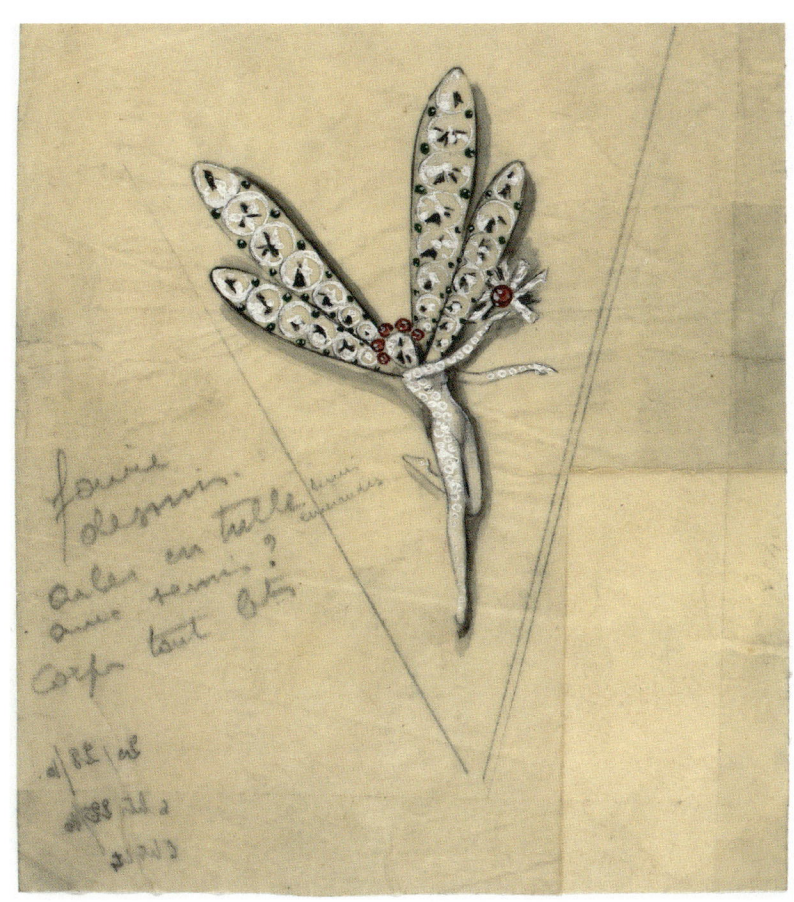

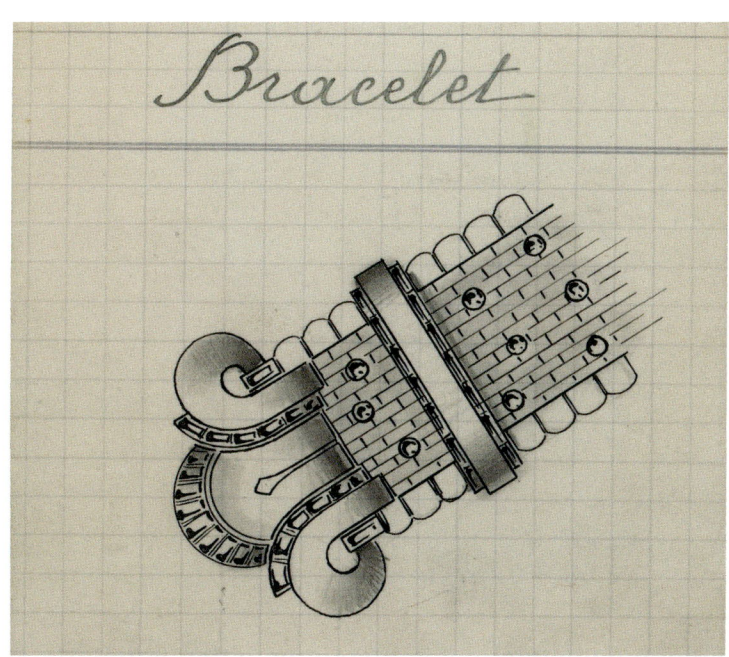

Clip of a little winged fairy in platinum, emeralds, rubies and diamonds by Van Cleef & Arpels, 1941. Ludo bracelet in platinum and diamonds by Van Cleef & Arpels, 1935.

Grand Duchess Vladimir's emeralds

In February 1917, the tsarist regime fell. A few months later, the youngest son of Grand Duchess Vladimir, aunt of Tsar Nicholas II, and a British diplomat played burglars, sneaking into the family palace by night to relieve its safe of the jewels belonging to the grand duchess, who was then in exile. Wrapped in newspaper, the treasure was stuffed into two Gladstone bags and sent to London in a diplomatic bag. Its sale would allow the grand duchess and her four children to live comfortably in exile in France. One of the main pieces, a sautoir necklace set with enormous emeralds, was acquired by the Chicago magnate Harold McCormick for his wife Edith, whose father was John D Rockefeller. When she died in 1932, the emeralds were dismantled and sold to Cartier for some $480,000. Barbara Hutton paid twice that for them and asked the House of Cartier to make a ring, earrings and a necklace from them. The latter contained the largest stone — weighing no less than 100 carats — which had probably belonged to Catherine the Great of Russia. In 1947, after a stay in India, Hutton asked the same jeweller to design a necklace that could be converted into a tiara in the Indian style. In 1967, she sold the jewel to Van Cleef & Arpels, which set the stones into several pieces of jewellery.

Grand Duchess Vladimir attends a ball at the Russian court in 1903, wearing her fabulous emeralds, which would be re-mounted by Cartier in 1936 and again in 1947 and bought by Barbara Hutton. In 1962, a frame was made so that the necklace could also be worn as a tiara. These emeralds have since been remounted on various pieces of jewellery by Van Cleef & Arpels.

Barbara Hutton wearing the Grand Duchess Vladimir's emeralds, mounted as a tiara by Cartier, photographed by Cecil Beaton in her palace, Sidi Hosni, in Tangier, Morocco, in 1962.

ALL CHANGE FOR ROYAL JEWELLERY

Diana, Princess of Wales

During her fifteen years as the Princess of Wales, Diana made her mark. Right down to her choice of jewellery, she showed how much she was an independent, modern woman.

Princess Diana wears the choker necklace consisting of seven strands of pearls fastened by a clasp adorned with an enormous Ceylon sapphire at a gala event, 20 November 1995. An iconic jewel, forever associated with the 'revenge dress' she wore in June 1994.

On 29 July 1981, 'the wedding of the century' – as the world's media called it – took place in St Paul's Cathedral in London. On the arm of her father, the 8th Earl Spencer, twenty-year-old Diana took three and a half minutes to walk down the red carpet of the aisle before the enraptured gaze of an estimated 750 million television viewers.

Royal reporters commented on her porcelain complexion, her 8-metre (25-foot) train, her pearly white smile and, of course, her impeccable lineage – the Spencers had been one Britain's most illustrious aristocratic families since the sixteenth century and both her grandmothers were or had been ladies-in-waiting to the queen mother. No one mentioned that the couple had met only thirteen times, or that the wedding had almost been blown to smithereens a few days earlier when Diana had discovered the existence of the prince's long-term girlfriend, Camilla Parker Bowles, a married woman to boot. Although the young bride seemed docile and malleable, she nevertheless managed to impose her will by choosing for her wedding a tiara from the Spencer jewel case, whereas tradition demanded that she wear a diadem from the Royal Collection. This choice was not insignificant: Diana, while becoming a Windsor, intended also to remain a Spencer and an independent woman.

This jewel, made up of scrolls and floral motifs in diamonds, had been designed in the eighteenth century. Originally more modest in form, it was remodelled and enriched in 1937 by the London jeweller Garrard at the request of Cynthia, Countess Spencer, Diana's paternal grandmother. A family treasure par excellence, the tiara was also worn by Lady Diana's sisters, Jane and Sarah, at their own weddings. Diana herself wore it on many occasions until 1992, the year of her separation from the Prince of Wales, after which she gave up wearing tiaras. Today, this Spencer tiara is the property of Charles, 9th Earl Spencer, although Prince William has agreed with his uncle that one day it will be handed down to his daughter, Princess Charlotte.

The marriage of Charles and Diana, 29 July 1981. Contrary to tradition, Diana is not wearing a diadem belonging to the royal family but a tiara from her own family, the Spencers.

At the British embassy in Washington, 1 November 1985, the Princess of Wales wears the Lover's Knot diadem given to her by the Queen on her marriage — a historic jewel, which she would return after her divorce.

The most famous engagement ring in the world

On 24 February 1981, in Buckingham Palace, a nineteen-year-old woman dressed in blue walked forward, shyly and awkwardly, on the arm of Prince Charles, thirteen years her senior. A journalist asked the future bridegroom a banal (and stupid) question, namely: were they in love? When Diana responded 'Of course!', Charles added 'Whatever "in love" means.' The beautiful, naive young woman looked decidedly uncomfortable, while the camera lingered insistently on her left ring finger, revealing her engagement ring to the world: an imposing oval marguerite made up of a central Ceylon sapphire of about 12 carats (royal tradition demands that the stone's weight should not be divulged) surrounded by fourteen diamonds in rows set in white gold. Some say Diana picked it from a choice of fifteen Garrard creations because it reminded her of her mother's engagement ring. Others maintain that the queen herself commissioned the ring, inspired by a wedding brooch given by Albert to Queen Victoria in 1840. The price was supposedly £28,000 — a trifle compared to most of the jewels in the Royal Collection. Five years later the flamboyant Sarah Ferguson would choose, for her engagement to Prince Andrew, a very similar ring featuring a central ruby. This marguerite motif chosen by Diana became the style desired by women around the world who got engaged in the 1980s. The ring was therefore endlessly copied, including in low-cost versions. In 1997, on Diana's death, Prince William inherited this ring, and planned to give it to his future wife when the time came. In 2010, he is said to have carried the precious jewel in a backpack for a week on a trip to Kenya with Catherine (Kate) Middleton, at the end of which he proposed marriage. Some time later, in a TV interview, the prince explained that this highly symbolic present was a way of keeping his mother close to him.

During the 1980s women all over the world dreamed of wearing this sapphire and diamond ring.
In 2010, William gave Diana's ring to Catherine, his fiancée, in a highly symbolic gesture.

THE WEIGHT OF ROYALTY

As official banquets and iconic portraits – notably the one commissioned by *Vogue* in 1990 – succeeded one another, one tiara was especially emblematic of the Princess of Wales: the Lover's Knot given to her by Queen Elizabeth on the occasion of her wedding. This imposing family treasure, consisting of nineteen inverted arcs surmounted by knots encrusted with diamonds from which hang pear-shaped pearls, was commissioned in 1913 from the jeweller Garrard for Queen Mary, who for its making sacrificed jewels inherited from her mother. Although highly appreciative of this tiara, Diana regularly complained of its weight, which she said gave her migraines, as well as of the constant sound made by the pearls swinging under their diamond hoops. On the announcement of her divorce from Prince Charles in 1996, Diana returned the jewel to Queen Elizabeth. It was to lie in the coffers of Buckingham Palace for almost two decades before Prince William's wife, Catherine, wore it in 2015, and several times since then.

SAPPHIRES AS BLUE AS HER EYES

The wedding of any princess or queen attracts a bevy of dazzling gifts. The most fabulous of these came from Crown Prince Fahd of Saudi Arabia: a set of jewels from the London jeweller Asprey worthy of *The Arabian Nights*. While these jewels were supposed to match the engagement ring given to Diana by Prince Charles, needless to say the latter piece paled in comparison. The suite comprised a pendant consisting of a sizeable Burmese sapphire set with baguette diamonds, suspended from a diamond rivière; a bracelet with two strands of diamonds and a sapphire cabochon, and a matching watch. The princess soon transformed part of the original set: the watch was dismantled to make earrings, and a choker necklace on a blue velvet ribbon was also made, which she wore at a Welsh charity ball in 1985. More daringly, Diana wore it as a headband at an official dinner held on 12 May 1986 in Tokyo by Japan's Emperor Hirohito.

Diana's relationship with her sapphires – which went so perfectly with her big blue eyes – was a love story of its own. A choker necklace was one of the most extravagant demonstrations of this: seven strands of pearls held together by a clasp made up of diamonds and a Sri Lankan sapphire as big as a duck egg – the latter having been originally been part of a brooch given to her as a wedding present by the queen mother. The choker, designed by the princess herself, made history when she famously wore it at the White House in 1985 when she took to the dance floor with actor John Travolta. And it later became a declaration of independence when she paired it with the daringly sexy 'revenge dress', only a few hours after Prince Charles had admitted on television to his adultery with Camilla.

EMERALDS OF TRANSGRESSION

Also in 1985, in Melbourne this time, Diana caused a sensation when she appeared wearing a dress of green taffeta, her forehead encircled by an extravagant headband of emeralds and diamonds. This unusual way of wearing a jewelled necklace seemed somewhat cavalier to purists, but Diana knew what she liked and was wont to have jewels she felt were too large for her taste dismantled in order to extract from them more discreet and modern clips or pendants. This Art Deco piece was made in 1921 out of an older necklace – the fabulous emerald and diamond Delhi Durbar Parure created by Garrard for Queen Mary on the occasion of her enthronement as Empress of India in 1911, alongside her husband, King George VI. Elizabeth II, who inherited Queen Mary's entire collection of jewels, agreed to lend this emerald necklace to Diana for life on her marriage, and it was one of the last pieces of jewellery the princess wore in public, on 1 July 1997, her thirty-sixth birthday, at a gala celebrating the centenary of London's Tate Gallery. On her death a few weeks later, the piece was returned to the queen, reappearing only after the latter's death in December 2022, now around Catherine's neck. As the new Princess of Wales was attending an environmental prizegiving, it was a highly symbolic choice – she dressed in green and wore green jewellery. Queen Mary's necklace had almost become an environmentalist banner. Jewels never cease to evolve and convey new meanings and messages.

In Australia in 1983, Diana wears the Spencer diadem, and the sapphire and diamond parure matching her engagement ring, given to her on her marriage by Crown Prince Fahd of Saudi Arabia.

JEWELS AS MYSTERIOUS AS THEY WERE COVETED

The Firm, as the British royal family is often known, has always enforced its rules and customs in every area, including dress and jewellery, but Diana had the audacity to be different. Along the way, both despite and because of her successive traumas and revolts, she raised herself to the status of fashion icon. While the queen favoured a wardrobe of bright colours at her official engagements, so as to be always visible to her people, Diana always chose to wear big jewels when she visited the bedsides of sick children in hospital, saying that she wore them for the young patients to play with. She was especially fond of large pearls, either on a necklace or as earrings, which she wore in a much more modern manner than her mother-in-law, who was usually seen sporting more severe-looking double and triple strands. One of the last sets of jewellery made for Diana by Garrard, dubbed the Swan Lake Suite, comprised five exceptional 12-mm South Sea pearls and 178 diamonds: fourteen marquise diamonds for the necklace and thirty-six diamonds for the earrings. She wore the whole set only once, on 3 June 1997, with an exquisite sky-blue minidress, at a performance of *Swan Lake* at the Royal Albert Hall in London. That same evening, it appears, the Egyptian businessman Mohammed Al-Fayed invited her to spend part of the summer at his property in the south of France, and there, fatefully, she would meet his son Dodi, the last man in her life. Garrard sold the suite to a British businessman, who later sold it to an extremely rich Texan, who sold it in 2011 to a couple of Ukrainian millionaires – who, in turn, offered it for sale in June 2023 in order to help finance the reconstruction of their war-torn country.

To date, only one other jewel worn by Princess Diana has been sold at auction: the Attallah Cross. This sale would have gone almost unnoticed had

Handed down from generation to generation, from Queen Mary, grandmother of Elizabeth II, to Catherine, Duchess of Cambridge, the extraordinary Delhi Durbar emeralds, mounted in 1921 by the jeweller Garrard.

The Princess of Wales herself wears Queen Mary's emerald and diamond choker at a banquet at Mansion House, 21 June 1989.

In June 1997, Diana attended a performance of *Swan Lake* at the Royal Albert Hall in London, wearing a pearl and diamond necklace and earrings designed for the occasion by Garrard. The set was due to be completed, but the princess tragically died two months later.

the buyer of this 1920s jewel by Garrard not been Kim Kardashian. Fetching a price of £163,800 (approximately $197,450), this dramatic pendant measures 13.6 by 9.5cm (5⅓ by 3¾in) and is set with eleven square amethysts and round diamonds. Diana wore the cross only once, at a London charity gala on 27 October 1987, teamed with an extravagant black-and-purple Elizabethan-style dress crowned by a ruff. The jewel had been lent to her by its owner, the Palestinian-British businessman Naim Attallah, who was then head of the House of Asprey & Garrard.

Finally, a very special ring featured in the last hours of Diana's life: the Dis-Moi Oui ('Say yes to me') model by Repossi, which Diana and Dodi Al-Fayed had set their hearts on after seeing it in the Italian jeweller's shop in Monaco on 10 August 1997. Alberto Repossi had offered to improve the jewel and send it on to the couple in Paris on 30 August. 'Diana seemed to like the youthful, modern and uncluttered aspect of our creations, which contrasted with the retro one of her royal jewels,' he later recalled. On the fateful day, only a few hours before the terrible car accident that cost the couple their lives, two rings were in fact delivered. Later, one of the two was supposedly returned to the jeweller, while the other one never reappeared. Mohammed Al-Fayed claimed that it remained locked up with the deceased couple's love letters in a safe in Switzerland. No one will ever know whether this Dis-Moi Oui model really was an engagement ring.

Diana in 1987, wearing an Elizabethan-style dress, and an astonishing pearl sautoir from which hangs the imposing Attallah Cross in amethysts and diamonds, made in the 1920s.

When Kate and Meghan wore Diana's jewels

In recent years, royal commentators have frequently indulged in a little game: spotting Diana's jewellery on her two daughters-in-law. On their mother's death in 1997, William and Harry inherited her entire jewellery collection and, once they were married, gave certain pieces to their respective wives. While Catherine usually wears Diana's royal jewels — the Lover's Knot tiara, a pair of pearl earrings with pendants, an emerald necklace, a bracelet with three strands of pearls, and, of course, her sapphire-and-diamond engagement ring, Meghan borrows more from her mother-in-law's day-to-day jewellery. Incidentally, Meghan's engagement ring, designed by Harry, features two diamonds from a brooch that once belonged to Diana. Meghan, who has made no secret of her admiration for this mother-in-law she never knew, has appeared several times wearing one of Diana's rings surmounted by a 30-carat emerald-cut aquamarine, notably at her wedding reception. Diana had herself ordered it from the jeweller Asprey the day after her separation, intending to wear it on her left ring finger as a replacement for her wedding and engagement rings. Meghan was first seen wearing a pair of butterfly earrings and a gold bracelet from Diana's collection in October 2018, a few hours after her first pregnancy was announced. It is also not uncommon for her to wear Diana's yellow gold Cartier Tank Française watch, or a superb diamond tennis bracelet, notably in March 2021 during the interview with Oprah Winfrey in which she accused the royal family of having racist attitudes. To show off a jewel once worn by the rebel princess who had been the bane of the House of Windsor thirty years earlier was quite a statement.

A jewel connects these two photographs, which are three decades apart: a ring adorned with an emerald-cut aquamarine gem. Meghan, Prince Harry's wife, wears it at Windsor Castle, 19 May 2018.

THE LAST CROWN JEWELS

Eugénie de Montijo

Empress Eugénie, who was born in 1826 and died in 1920, endured fifty years of exile. She witnessed the invention of photography and the cinema and lived through the First World War. A jewellery fanatic, she was also the last to wear the French crown jewels. Hers was a sparkling collection of jewellery before the fading of the imperial light.

The empress with some of her innumerable pearls, painted by Franz Xaver Winterhalter in 1853.

On 24 June 1872 in London, Christie's offered for sale a portion of a private collection of jewellery belonging to 'a distinguished Lady'. Although the name of the lady was withheld, it was an open secret that the owner was Empress Eugénie, who had been living in exile in England since the fall of the Second Empire two years earlier. There were 123 lots, comprising, notably, two strands of marvellous pearls and part of an exceptional collection of Colombian emeralds. Examples of the latter, bequeathed to Eugénie's goddaughter Queen Victoria Eugénie of Spain, would resurface a century later in Iran, around the neck of Farah Pahlavi, wife of the last shah. But most of the pieces sold would, over decades, end up in the possession of a great admirer of the empress, Aimée de Heeren, an extremely wealthy Brazilian socialite and collector who was born in 1903 and died, aged 103, in 2006. In May 1887, another auction, in Paris, saw the demise of the entire treasure of the French Crown, the Third Republic having decided that the dispersal of the former royal and imperial jewels would remove from the French people any temptation to return to hereditary rule. It was a giant clearance sale which enabled newly wealthy industrialists, American above all, to acquire the relics of the country's royal past, some of them dating back as far as the reign of the Renaissance king Francis I.

A NEED TO SHINE

Louis-Napoleon Bonaparte, nephew of Napoleon I, was still the president of the Second Republic when in 1848, at the home of his cousin Mathilde Bonaparte, he met Eugénie-Marie de Montijo, Countess of Teba, a Spanish and Bonapartist aristocrat who owed her totally French education to two illustrious teachers: the novelist Stendhal for history and the poet Prosper Mérimée for the French language. The young woman was deeply pious, very beautiful and highly elegant but, it was said, preoccupied by the impression she made, a little too emancipated, and given to intrigue. An assiduous courtship followed, notably featuring an idyllic stay in the Château de Compiègne, Oise, in the autumn of 1852. On a morning walk in the park among dew-covered lawns, Eugénie spotted a magnificent clover leaf; to her, it looked as sparkling as a diamond pendant. Captivated by the young woman, Napoleon III immediately entrusted Count Baciocchi with the mission of finding a jewel that reproduced such beauty. This delicate clover-shaped brooch of emeralds and diamonds would become one of Eugénie's most cherished jewels, and she wore it all her life, on formal occasions as well as with more simple garments.

The imperial wedding took place in Notre-Dame, Paris, on 29 January 1853, and was an opportunity

A peacock feather brooch in diamonds, sapphires, emeralds and rubies, commissioned by the empress from the jeweller Mellerio.

Shortly after her wedding, Empress Eugénie commissioned Fossin to make a portrait brooch (most likely along with that of Napoleon III) surrounded by rays of diamonds and topped with a green enamel and diamond clover leaf. This green enamel clover leaf, separated from the brooch — the fate of which is unknown — is now preserved in the heritage collection of the House of Chaumet.

Miniature portrait of Empress Eugénie. She is wearing a set of pearls and the sapphire diadem from the crown jewels.

The empress kneeling at a prie-dieu in the chateau of Saint-Cloud, photographed by Gustave Le Gray.

for Eugénie to introduce herself to the French people. She was bedecked with jewellery: corsages and frogging studded with diamonds; belt, diadem and hair combs of sapphires and diamonds; pearl necklace and more. Anxious that his reign should be as glittering as that of his uncle Napoleon I, Louis-Napoleon Bonaparte, now Napoleon III, was heedless of the expense: he squandered the equivalent of £25.7 million or $34.5 million on jewellery in just the first six months of 1853. Gabriel Lemonnier, a very prominent jeweller and one of the court's official suppliers, delivered a parure of rubies and fine pearls, another of sapphires and diamonds, another of grey pearls, and yet another of fine pearls and emeralds – the empress's favourite precious stone. Until then, the emperor's private family jewellery collection had been scanty, his mother, Hortense de Beauharnais, having been obliged to sell almost all her jewels. Nevertheless, there remained a very fine series of *épi de blé* rings with diamonds and the so-called Talisman of Charlemagne that enchanted Eugénie. This golden reliquary medallion set with 150 precious stones, a sapphire of 190 carats, and a glass cabochon containing a fragment of the True Cross, had supposedly been given to the emperor by the Abbasid caliph Harun al-Rashid in 801. It was given to Napoleon Bonaparte and Joséphine in 1804, and subsequently bequeathed to the latter's daughter, Hortense. A few months before her death, Eugénie donated it to Reims Cathedral, where it has been kept ever since.

A PASSION FOR PEARLS

Far removed from the restraint of the Citizen King, Louis-Philippe I, Napoleon III revived all the ostentation of the French Empire and opened up the treasury of the French Crown so that Eugénie, who had a voracious appetite for jewellery, could take her pick. At her disposal were, notably, parures that had belonged to Marie Thérèse of France, eldest daughter of Louis XVI and Marie Antoinette, most of which

Eugénie wears the La Régente pearl, also known as La Perle de Napoléon, attached to a ribbon as a choker. This teardrop-shaped natural saltwater pearl, the size of a pigeon egg, weighs 302.68 grains. Here it is shown with a pair of natural pearl earrings.

she had dismantled and refashioned into the most extravagant jewellery in the contemporary taste – her 'harnesses of power' as she called them. The empress avowed a great passion for Marie Antoinette and the eighteenth-century style more generally, and accordingly wanted to bring back into fashion hooped petticoats, flounces, bows, garlands and other rococo adornments. Her jewellery collection reflected this nostalgia. From the jewellers Alfred Bapst and Jean-François Mellerio she ordered a large number of jewelled belts – including a remarkable adjustable one featuring currant leaves – shoulder bows, corsages, and roses and stars to be pinned in the hair – all encrusted with diamonds. Another large belt attracted particular attention: designed in 1864, it featured sixty-three pearls, ten amethysts, eight emeralds, four sapphires, four pink topazes, six yellow topazes, a spinel and a ruby. To these was added a *berthe en résille* studded with a thousand and one stones, a jewelled net that covered the throat and shoulders. This excess soon earned the empress the unflattering sobriquets of *Falbala I* ('Frill the First') and *Fée Chiffon* ('Rag Fairy').

The numerous portraits of the empress, and especially the numerous photographs of her taken by Michel Berthaud on the occasion of the sale of the French crown jewels in 1887, convey the extent and extravagance of the imperial jewellery collection. In the portrait painted by Édouard Dubufe in 1853, which still hangs in the Château de Compiègne, Eugénie is adorned with cascades of pearls: pear-shaped pendants worn at the base of the neck, a long four-strand sautoir of 366 pearls (she also owned another, eight-strand one with 542 pearls), four-strand cuff bracelets on each wrist and, in the hollow of her décolletage, the famous clover leaf by Fossin. For her wedding she received a brooch of flowers and leaves in pearls and diamonds by Alexandre-Gabriel Lemonnier, in the centre of which La Régente – a fabulous pear-shaped pearl of 302.68 grains, the size of a pigeon egg – took pride of place. At the time, La Régente was perhaps the biggest natural pearl in the world, purchased by Napoleon Bonaparte for his second wife, Empress Marie-Louise. La Régente was bought in the 1887 state sale by the jeweller Gustav Fabergé, who mounted it in a pendant and sold it on to the Russian aristocrat Prince Nicholas Yusupov as a gift for his daughter, Princess Zinaida. After being seized by the Bolsheviks, it was then resold numerous times, without its origin being known. Finally, in 1987, its imperial provenance was established; in 2005, its sale by Christie's in Geneva broke all records at $2.5 million.

THE LAST GLIMMERS OF THE ANCIENT WORLD

The powerful rivalry between Empress Eugénie and her husband's cousin Princess Mathilde forced jewellers to push the boundaries of their genius. Both women – who hated each other ever since the first stole the heart of the emperor at the expense of the second – went to Mellerio at 22 Rue de la Paix twice a week to demand ever more innovative and

A heart-shaped pendant encrusted with rubies and diamonds, with on the reverse side a glazed compartment containing a lock of the hair of Emperor Napoleon III.

A collection of jewels that belonged to Empress Eugénie: shown in its case, a pair of currant leaf earrings made by Bapst Frères in 1855, together with their matching brooch; a second brooch, shown in its case, in gold and silver, encrusted with diamonds, an emerald and pearls, by Bapst Frères in 1864; and finally a third brooch consisting of three currant leaves from which hang three jointed and detachable tapered pendants.

Eugénie de Montijo

opulent jewels. After a passion for botanical motifs came inspiration from the antique world, which proved a game-changer. The House of Bapst created the finest example – a Greek diadem at the centre of which was the Regent, a diamond of 140 carats taken from the French crown jewels. This legendary stone owed its name to Philippe d'Orléans, brother of Louis XIV, who had acquired it. It featured in the coronation crown of Louis XV in 1722, and was later used to decorate one of Marie-Antoinette's hats. Subsequently, Napoleon had it set into the sword used at his coronation as Emperor of the French in 1804. Other major diamonds from the treasure – the Hortensia, the Huitième Mazarin and the Florentine Diamond – were also requisitioned by Eugénie to adorn a comb designed for the baptism of the prince imperial and worn at the back of her chignon. The fashion for the Antique became even more accentuated when the emperor bought the extraordinary Giampietro Campana collection, which today is a one of the star exhibits in the Louvre – a selection of Italian Renaissance paintings and statues, Greek and Etruscan ceramics, and a fabulous collection of ancient jewellery. The empress, beguiled by the fashion of the time, did not hesitate to adorn her hair with an Etruscan comb, and her forehead with a band set with eight cameos in pink coral.

As regent during the Franco-Prussian War in 1870–1, Eugénie was the last woman to govern France. On 2 September, the emperor was taken prisoner at Sedan, in the Ardennes; the Second Empire fell and the empress had to flee Paris. Her flight, made possible with the help of her dentist, was notable for her ladies-in-waiting hastily stuffing the luggage of the Duchess of Malakoff and Madame Pollet, the empress's treasurer, full of jewels. The jewels were then hidden in a chest of drawers belonging to the Princess von Metternich before being deposited for safekeeping at the Bank of England, from where Eugénie, in exile in England, would eventually retrieve them. She died in 1920, exactly fifty years after being dethroned.

Portrait of the empress wearing an antique-style diadem, by Franz Xaver Winterhalter (1862).

Extracts from the Berthaud catalogue published in 1887 in preparation for the great auction of the crown jewels, which was held in the Louvre from 12 to 23 May. A symbolic act decreed by the Third Republic, it was both a financial failure and a squandering of heritage. The jewels of the French monarchs were thus scattered, bought at very low prices by noble jewellery houses and very wealthy Americans.

Eugénie de Montijo

The Louvre – a fine jewellery case

The empress's crown, made by Alexandre-Gabriel Lemonnier, was miraculously spared from the auction of 1887, so it never left the Louvre. The crown was adorned with suitably imperial motifs, featuring eight hoops in the shape of eagles' wings, which joined together beneath a globe encrusted with diamonds and surmounted by a cross, itself adorned with six diamonds. This crown, the last made for a French monarch, comprised 2,490 diamonds and 56 emeralds. For several decades, the Société des amis du Louvre (Friends of the Louvre) has taken steps to bring together and exhibit pieces from the French crown jewels. One of Eugénie's most fabulous diadems was a fortunate example. It was made by Lemonnier in 1853 from a jewel created by Marie-Étienne Nitot, founder of the House of Chaumet, for Empress Marie-Louise. This exceptional piece of head jewellery, comprising 1,998 diamonds and 212 pearls, was acquired in 1887 by the jeweller Jacoby, then in 1890 by the German prince Albert von Thurn und Taxis. The latter's descendants kept it for a century before selling it to the Louvre in 1992. Finally, two of Empress Eugénie's brooches also found their way to the Louvre: in 2015, a shoulder brooch of pearls and diamonds; and before that, in 2008, a large corsage made in 1855 by François Kramer. In 1887, this extraordinary piece, made up of 2,438 diamonds, became the property of the jeweller Émile Schlesinger, who sold it on to the extremely wealthy American Caroline Astor. It later appeared in the coffers of the Duke of Westminster, then in those of the Earls Beauchamp and the American jeweller Ralph Esmerian, before finally finding its place in a display case in the Louvre.

Four of the empress's jewels are now on display at the Louvre: a pearl and diamond shoulder brooch, a diamond bodice bow, a pearl and diamond tiara, and an imperial crown, the last one ever made for a French monarch.

THE JEWELS OF EXILE

The Duchess of Windsor

She dreamed of becoming queen, but while she got the jewels, she never ascended the throne. The Duke of Windsor lavished enormous sums on Wallis Simpson, while jewellers vied with each other in designing and offering her inventive, modern pieces. Her collection was a treasure that, until its dispersal, was the subject of speculation and gossip.

Wallis, Duchess of Windsor, née Simpson, richly adorned and wearing the 'Monkey Dress' by Hubert de Givenchy, photographed in the lounge of the Villa Windsor, on the edge of the Bois de Boulogne.

Wallis Simpson trailed in her wake the pungent whiff of scandal. This American divorcee possessed neither great beauty nor pedigree, yet she managed to shake the British Crown like no other interloper before her. On 11 December 1936, King Edward VIII – known by another of his birth names, David, to his family – announced his abdication, just under eleven months after he had ascended the throne. And the reason he gave was his love for a twice-divorced woman from an impoverished background in Baltimore. The couple had first met at a shooting weekend in January 1931, when she was still married to her second husband and he was still the Prince of Wales, and quickly formed a deep and obsessive relationship. Wallis saw herself as a future queen and empress, but had to make do with exile after the scandal of their affair erupted and he was forced to abdicate and take the title of Duke of Windsor. It was a gilded exile, admittedly – and a glittering one, given the duke's fortune and a private casket filled with exceptional precious stones. Madly in love, and at the mercy of a woman reputed to be hard and calculating, the duke ceaselessly tried to make up to his wife for the affront of exile, by means of sumptuous jewels and suites of jewellery created exclusively for her.

THE JEWELS OF LOVE

'I'm not a beautiful woman. I'm nothing to look at, so the only thing I can do is dress better than anyone else,' the Duchess of Windsor once told a friend. And in that she excelled. Wearing Chanel, Schiaparelli, Poiret and Givenchy, she appeared on the International Best Dressed List Hall of Fame for sixteen successive years, from 1941 to 1957. Her sartorial flair was inseparable from her taste for jewellery. Hubert de Givenchy even asked her to come to his home with her latest jewellery acquisitions so

Design drawings for various jewels belonging to the duchess: a ring in gold, coral, emeralds and diamonds, Cartier Paris, 1947; a ring in platinum, sapphires and diamonds, Cartier, 1949; and a heart-shaped brooch in gold, platinum, emeralds, rubies and diamonds, given by the duke to his wife for their twentieth wedding anniversary, Cartier, 1957.

Design drawing for a diamond, sapphire, and platinum necklace, Cartier, 1951.

The Duchess of Windsor wearing one of her most emblematic jewels: a Cartier diamond charm bracelet with nine gem-set crosses, each representing an event in the duke and duchess's life together and engraved with a message.

he could create a dress that would showcase them. When it came to standing out in society, Wallis had no equal. Elegance lay in the details: she adorned herself with sapphires when in the blue dining room of her Bois de Boulogne mansion and with yellow diamonds when in the library with its saffron-coloured sofa. Although she had been refused the title of Her Royal Highness, the duchess made clothes and jewellery the tools of her power instead.

But the duchess's jewels also expressed love – or that of the duke, at least. Indeed, inscribed on many of them was a word or short phrase evoking a memory, anniversary or sentiment. It was a custom dear to the duke, no doubt echoing a tradition started by Prince Albert, who had his words of love engraved on the jewellery he gave to Queen Victoria. A chain bracelet with circular- and brilliant-cut diamonds, hung with nine gem-set Latin crosses, perhaps illustrates more than any other piece the ties that bound the Duke and Duchess of Windsor. On the back of each cross was an inscription containing their names plus a date. The first of these read 'WE [a pun on Wallis/Edward] are too 25-XI-34', implying 'We too are in love' in an allusion to the marriage of the duke's brother, the Duke of Kent, which had taken place a few days later. Another engraving mentioned the appendectomy Wallis had undergone. And on the last of the nine crosses was the date of their marriage, 3 June 1937. Wallis wore the bracelet on her left wrist, the same side as her heart and wedding ring, on the day she married the duke. Years later, the French singer Mireille Mathieu would be spotted several times wearing this piece.

On the bride's right wrist that day was a much more impressive Jarretière bracelet, given to her by the duke in May 1937, shortly before their wedding: a broad flexible band of brilliant-cut and baguette-cut diamonds with a clasp in the shape of a stylized knot with a pavé of cushion-cut sapphires and baguette diamonds. Several months before the duke, Marlene Dietrich had also bought a similar Jarretière bracelet, though hers featured a pavé of rubies.

The Duchess of Windsor 153

The Duke and Duchess of Windsor, photographed in 1941. She is wearing a Van Cleef & Arpels Bouquet brooch featuring clusters of sapphire and ruby flowers.

A STRONG SENSE OF MODERNITY

The Duchess of Windsor never had a taste for old jewels, preferring instead contemporary pieces from the 1930s to the 1950s. She was one of the first to wear high jewellery yellow-gold pieces, when platinum was still in fashion. During the war, gold was rationed and stockpiled, but from 1945 it regained its place in jewellers' palettes and imaginations. Like his wife, the duke was a great connoisseur of jewellery – a taste that doubtless came from his mother, Queen Mary, for whom he had always had the greatest admiration. A model of dapper elegance himself, and perfectionist to a fault, he was an assiduous follower of fashion and the latest trends and was the source of many (it is to him, for example, that we owe the terms 'Windsor knot' and 'Prince of Wales check').

In the 1930s, his taste for jewellery and his desire to satisfy his wife led him to spend long hours with Jeanne Toussaint, artistic director at Cartier, and Renée Puissant, who held the same post at Van Cleef & Arpels. Together, they designed avant-garde pieces that helped to revolutionize the style of modern jewellery. In particular, Renée Puissant was the originator of the Zip necklace, inspired by the appearance of the zip fastener. The outbreak of war delayed the design of the jewel and it came into existence only in 1950, eight years after Puissant had died by suicide. When open, the Zip is a necklace; when closed, it becomes a bracelet: a truly iconic piece by the House of Van Cleef & Arpels.

Among the creations of this house was a beautiful necklace of rubies and diamonds. A first, a relatively simple version was bought by the new king in 1936 for Simpson's fortieth birthday. This was an extremely painful period for the couple, when Edward's accession as Edward VIII forced him to keep away from Wallis as long as she was still married to Ernest Simpson. Three years later, when the couple were living in exile, the now Duke of Windsor completely redesigned the piece as intertwined ribbons of baguette diamonds and cushion-cut rubies with a *chute en drapé* (draped swag). On the clasp were the words: 'My Wallis from her David 19 VI 36'. The piece featured 123 Burmese rubies. In 1936, the gift was immediately followed by ivy-leaf earrings, a two-leaf brooch and a matching ruby bracelet engraved with the message 'Hold Tight 27-III-36', at a time when Wallis was pining for the king and enraged that the British Establishment was refusing to countenance their marriage. The same message had already appeared on a pair of diamond cufflinks given by Simpson to Edward the previous year.

Illustrations of the famous diamond and sapphire Jarretière bracelet by Van Cleef & Arpels, 1937, and for a double clip in sapphires and diamonds, 1938, by the same jewellery house.

EXTRAORDINARY STONES

Although many of the Duchess of Windsor's jewels were made from stones that had come from the royal family's collection, the couple also had a sixth sense for acquiring exceptional gems, such as the McLean diamond, which Wallis would wear as a ring – a cushion-cut stone of 31.26 carats which had previously belonged to the American socialite Evalyn Walsh McLean. Among the duchess's diamonds were also two pear-shaped canary-yellow diamond clips, one of 40.81 carats and the other of 52.13 carats. Swooning before them, Wallis hastened to write to the New York jeweller who had made them, Harry Winston, to ask whether he would be able to make earrings that could match them. Her wish was, of course, granted.

The emeralds in the Windsors' jewel case were equally fascinating. There was a gorgeous one of 48.95 carats, mounted in a pendant, which had belonged to the King Alfonso XIII of Spain, and a rectangular step-cut one that Edward had acquired in 1936 with the idea of making an engagement ring for the woman he could not yet marry. He had the words 'We are ours now' engraved on it and gave it to her on 27 October 1936, that same day on which she was summoned to a court hearing regarding her divorce from Ernest Simpson. This stone of 19.77 carats had supposedly once belonged to a Grand Mogul. It was the size of a duck egg until Cartier, considering it too expensive to resell, cut it in two. One part was bought by an American billionaire; the other by the man who at that point was still King of England. This gave Wallis a taste for emeralds. Thus in 1957 she treated herself to a magnificent necklace of Indian teardrop emeralds from Harry Winston. She wore it at a society party. Among the guests was the Maharani of Baroda, who recognized in this necklace two ankle bracelets that had been recently sold from the Baroda royal treasure. She declared, loudly enough for everyone to hear, that the duchess was wearing jewels she had once worn on her feet. Cut to the quick, the proud Wallis returned the necklace to the New York jeweller the next day.

In 1971, the Duke of Windsor was diagnosed with throat cancer and he died the following year. Wallis survived him by fourteen years, becoming a recluse in a mansion that was now deserted by the couple's friends, and going into steep cognitive decline that eventually cost her her speech. She nevertheless took care to bequeath her marvellous eighteenth-century furniture to the French State, terrified that it might be passed on to the British royal family, practically all of whom she hated. She died on 24 April 1986 in her Paris home. Her final revenge was to be buried as 'Wallis, Duchess of Windsor' by the side of her husband, in the Royal Burial Ground at Frogmore, close to the Royal Mausoleum of Queen Victoria and Prince Albert, a royal couple who, like the Windsors, had loved each other so deeply.

Bracelet in yellow gold, rose gold, platinum, diamonds, amethysts, and turquoise gemstones, Cartier, 1954.
The Duchess of Windsor wearing a drape necklace in platinum and yellow gold, with amethysts, diamonds and turquoise gemstones, commissioned from the House of Cartier in 1947 (see p.7).

Priceless little creatures

Wallis Simpson had a creative streak and, even more, a love of animals. Apart from her beloved pugs — she even had a pug-shaped gold handbag made — and her white organdie dress with its motif of lobsters sprinkled with parsley, designed for her by Elsa Schiaparelli and Salvador Dalí in the summer of 1937, she very often wore animal-themed jewellery, especially frogs — as seen in a rigid bracelet and a pair of earrings designed by David Webb in New York in 1964. The same designer also created no fewer than four pairs of shell earrings for the duchess. Her menagerie of pieces included a marvellous butterfly clip, as well as an exceptional flamingo brooch made under the creative direction of Jeanne Toussaint for Cartier in 1940. The plumage was decorated with emeralds, rubies and sapphires and the beak with two sapphire cabochons, while the bird's head, neck, body and legs were made of pavés of diamonds.

But nothing surpassed the feline pieces also designed by Jeanne Toussaint, pieces that today are iconic. The panther had made an appearance, in black onyx and white diamonds, on a watch by Cartier in 1914. Since the success of Rudyard Kipling's *Jungle Book* a few years earlier, the panther, with its exoticism and sleek agility, naturally found its way into Art Deco imagery. Toussaint, a close friend of Louis Cartier and future artistic director of the House of Cartier, sported an evening bag with a clasp surmounted by a panther in onyx and diamonds. It was enough to earn her the nickname Jeanne la Panthère. In 1948, she was visited by Wallis Simpson who, having recently been burgled, wanted to buy some new pieces. Accordingly, Toussaint designed a crouching panther perched on a cabochon emerald of considerable size — 116.74 carats. The duchess was so captivated that the following year she acquired a new panther — this one paved with diamonds and sapphires, and mounted on a fabulous cabochon sapphire of 152.35 carats. In 1952, the Cartier workshops surpassed themselves once more, creating a panther bracelet made entirely of diamonds and onyx, whose supple, slender, articulated body wrapped easily around the wrist — a true tour de force. Four years later, the duchess asked for a similar model in a tiger version, with its legs dangling and set with daffodil-yellow diamonds on yellow gold. With the addition of various clips and bracelets, the Windsor jewellery case included eight big cats — aptly, perhaps, for a woman always quick to bare her claws.

Pink flamingo brooch commissioned by the Duke of Windsor from the House of Cartier in March 1940; platinum, yellow gold, diamonds, emeralds, sapphires, rubies and citrine.

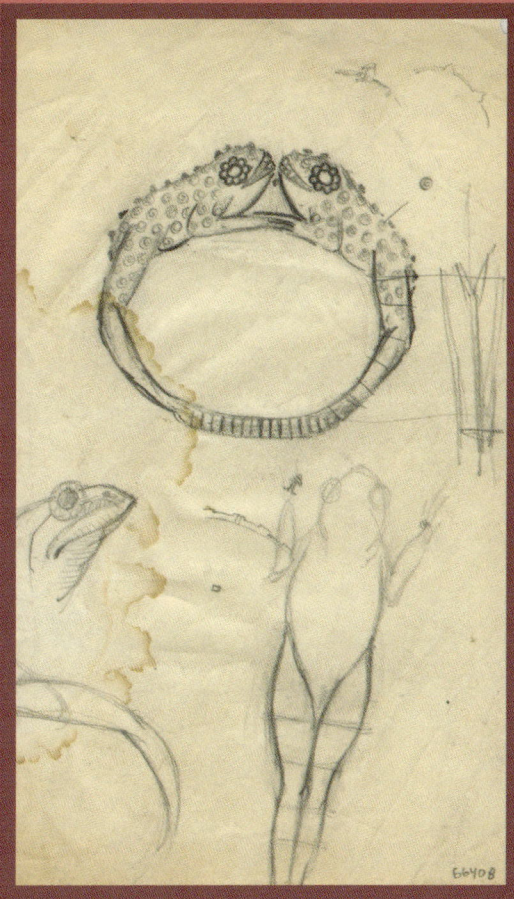

Design drawing for a panther bracelet made by Cartier in 1952: platinum, emeralds, onyx and diamonds; bracelet depicting a frog with two heads, by the American jeweller David Webb; and a panther brooch in gold and black enamel on an emerald cabochon, Cartier, 1948.

The Duchess of Windsor 159

The duchess in her Paris house, wearing a fabulous necklace of emeralds and diamonds made by Cartier in 1960. It features five pear-shaped motifs with, in its centre, a detachable pendant set with a pendeloque-cut emerald, which can be worn as a clip.

The sale of the century

On 2 and 3 April 1987, a year after her death, the cherished treasures of the Duchess of Windsor were dispersed. The world had its eyes riveted on a marquee erected in Geneva, on the quai du Mont-Blanc, facing Lake Geneva. A total of 1,500 potential buyers were crammed within, and 700 more were watching on screens in the Hôtel Beau Rivage. Sotheby's had accredited 250 journalists and 17 television crews — unprecedented for a jewel sale. An exhibition of the Duchess of Windsor's jewels in New York and then Palm Beach had already attracted extraordinary crowds, and on the day of the sale the world's most famous jewellers were there, as well as Nadine de Rothschild, Shirley Bassey and Baron and Baroness Thyssen-Bornemisza, plus many more on the telephone, including Elizabeth Taylor. The men wore tuxedos and the women were in evening gowns and heavily bejewelled. The bids soared, and the jewels fetched between five and thirty times their estimate, for a total of $45 million, equivalent to £68 million or $92 million today. Numerous jewellery houses bought back their creations in order to enrich their archives, while major collectors treated themselves to a piece of the Windsor legend. The proceeds of the sale were destined for the Institut Pasteur, to contribute to the fight against cancer and AIDS. The duchess had stipulated in her will that her legacy should not fund experiments on animals, but did not respect the wishes of the duke, who during his lifetime had asked that after the couple's deaths all the jewels should be removed from their mounts so that no other woman could wear them. Twenty-three years later, on 30 November 2013, at Sotheby's in London, twenty jewels from the collection came back up for sale, smashing new records. Thus the onyx-and-diamond panther bracelet sold for £4.5 million and the joyous flamingo brooch for £1.7 million.

A set of jewels by Suzanne Belperron: two bracelets, a necklace and earrings in blue chalcedony, sapphires and diamonds.

A set consisting of a necklace, bracelet and brooch with two feathers in diamonds and rubies, made by Van Cleef & Arpels between 1936 and 1939. Also shown are the heart-shaped brooch made by Cartier in 1957 and a ring by Harry Winston featuring a cushion-cut diamond of 31.26 carats, which had belonged to the American Evalyn Walsh McLean, owner of the famous Hope Diamond.

DIAMONDS ON THE RIVIERA

Grace Kelly

Like the heroine of a fairy tale, Grace Kelly went from the movie studios of Hollywood to the Prince's Palace of Monaco. In her wake, the Monegasque jewellery collection was elegantly enriched.

Princess Grace wearing two Van Cleef & Arpels jewels in the 1970s: a pair of diamond ear pendants of plant-inspired design, given to her by Prince Rainier, and a sapphire and diamond brooch.

In January 1956, Hollywood actor Grace Kelly was making what would be her last film, *High Society*, playing a young woman torn between two men – her new fiancé and her ex-husband. For her character's imposing engagement ring, the film's prop master unearthed a glass jewel of good size but lacking in brilliance. Grace Kelly insisted she wear a jewel of her own instead: her engagement ring – an emerald-cut diamond that Prince Rainier of Monaco had slipped onto her finger just a few weeks earlier. A fellow member of the cast, Celeste Holm, recalling the star's arrival on set with her diamond on her finger, said it was the size of an ice rink and marvelled at its extraordinary colour and liveliness. The 'rock' astonished everyone, but Kelly, always elegant and refined, is said to have merely replied that it was indeed 'charming'. 'Impressive' might have been more accurate, considering that it weighed 10.48 carats, measured 1.5 by 1.13cm (⅝ by ½in) and was set in a platinum mount by Cartier.

A POOR PRINCELY COLLECTION

When, during the 1955 Cannes Festival, the French magazine *Paris Match* proposed, for an article that was never published, a meeting in the Palace of Monaco between a Hollywood actor who had just won an Oscar and a thirty-year-old bachelor prince, then unknown in America, no woman had resided permanently in that palace for almost a century. The wife of Prince Albert I had fled Monaco in 1870 after barely a year of marriage; Prince Louis II waited until he was seventy-six before marrying his mistress; and his daughter Charlotte deserted the principality for France. With no women around, the palace's coffers lacked a jewellery collection of any size. And although Charlotte, Prince Rainier's mother, had been the first of the Grimaldi dynasty to acquire some very fine pieces of jewellery, she was in no mood to share them with this upstart daughter-in-law who had arrived from America to marry her son in April 1956.

The impressive Cartier engagement ring given to Grace Kelly by Prince Rainier in January 1956 — an emerald-cut diamond of 10.48 carats set in platinum.

A 1953 Cartier necklace consisting of baguette and round diamonds set in platinum and arranged in three garlands, given to Grace Kelly for her wedding by the principality's National Council. One of her favourite jewels, it has since been worn by her elder daughter, Princess Caroline.

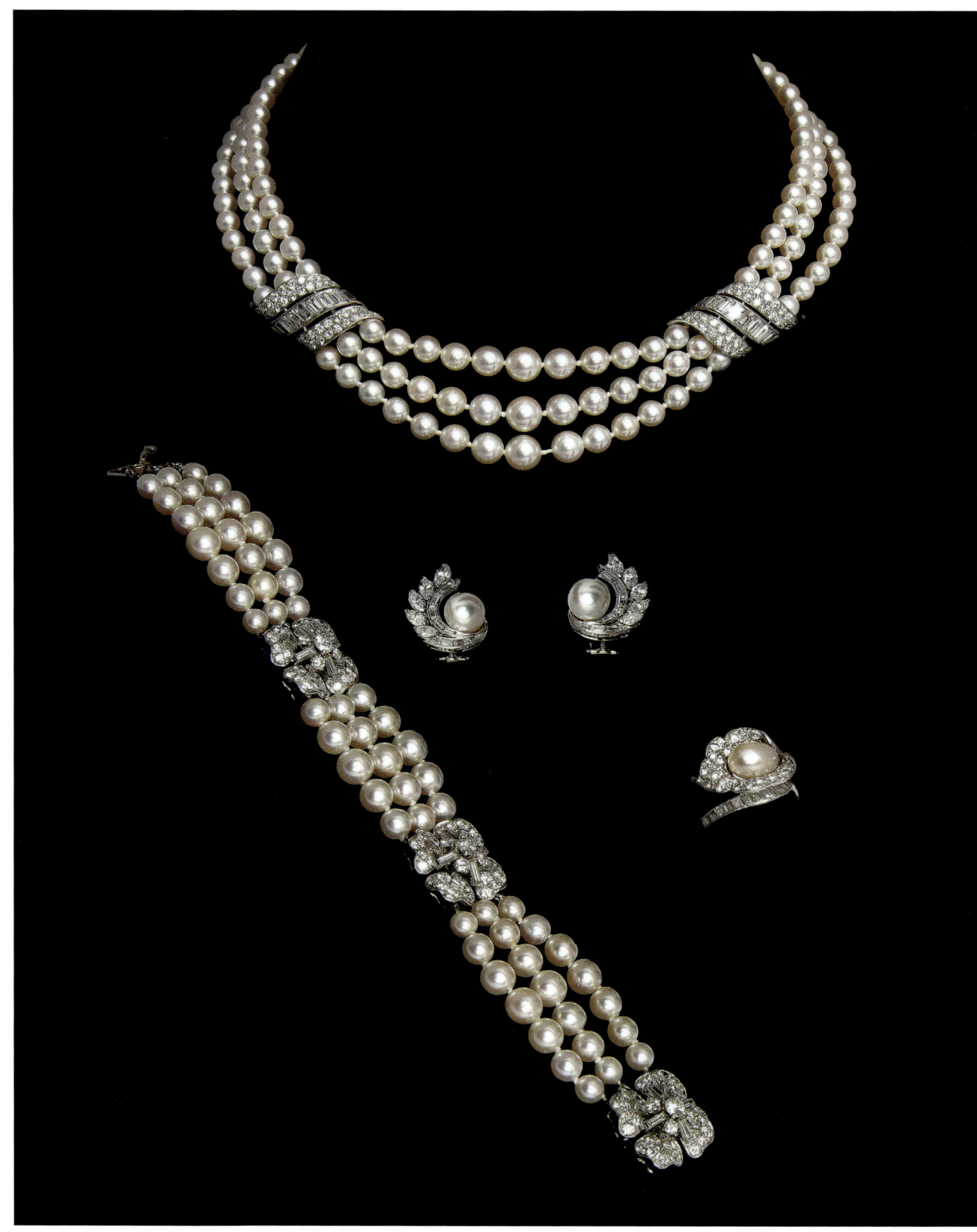

A set of pearl and diamond jewels by Van Cleef & Arpels — a wedding present from Prince Rainier: a necklace made up of three strands of pearls and baguette-cut and brilliant-cut diamonds, a ring in the shape of a lily, a bracelet of three strands of pearls with floral motifs, and earrings in pearls with diamond petals.

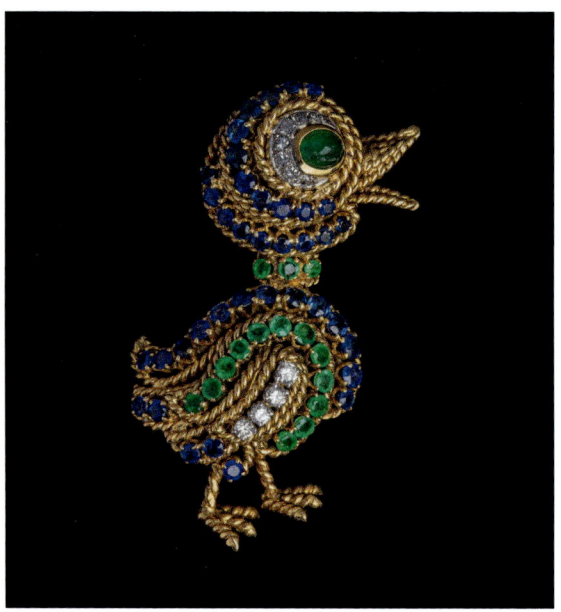 

Notable in Princess Charlotte's collection were two diadems. One, created by Cartier in 1949 on the accession of Rainier III, consisted of pear-shaped pearls and diamonds set in white gold and platinum. The other, of Kokoshnik-style diamond needles, was worn in 2005 as a necklace by Princess Caroline, Rainier and Grace's elder daughter, on the accession of her brother, Albert II. There was also a necklace of cabochon sapphires and diamonds. Princess Charlotte died in 1977, but Grace always refused to wear her mother-in-law's jewels, except for the pearl diadem which she wore just once. The reason was simple: there was a deep hostility between the two women. Only Princess Caroline – whom Grace pointedly did not name after her grandmother as tradition demanded – occasionally wore them.

THE DELICACY OF PEARLS

Lacking a jewellery collection worthy of the name, Grace received from the prince a very fine parure by Van Cleef & Arpels New York in January 1956, a few days before the official announcement of their engagement. It comprised a three-strand pearl necklace, the strands linked by two motifs of baguette and brilliant diamonds; a three-strand bracelet of pearls, the strands linked by three fleurettes encrusted with diamonds; earrings in navette diamonds and a ring featuring a lily of diamonds surmounted by a pear-shaped oriental pearl. Guided in his purchase by Louis Arpels himself – to match, Arpels said, Grace's delicate beauty – the prince made the jeweller the official supplier to the principality. The new princess first wore this pearl-and-diamond parure on her honeymoon, and then regularly over the years, especially in official portraits. 'I favour pearls on the screen and in my private life,' Grace is reputed to have said early in her acting career. At Van Cleef & Arpels, the prince also ordered some diamond earrings with a botanical motif, which years later would be worn by Princess Caroline and then by her daughter-in-law, Tatiana Santo Domingo.

Fond of sophisticated chignons, hair ornaments and other head jewellery, Grace also received from

Grace had a strong affinity with animals and possessed an adorable collection of animal jewels — notably this brooch depicting a Normandy duck, made by Van Cleef & Arpels in 1955 and acquired in 1956.

her husband a small diadem with festoons, set with diamonds. A collection of 214 modern-cut diamonds and 42 baguette-cut diamonds mounted in platinum, this diadem was the one Grace wore most often at official ceremonies, notably at the wedding of King Juan Carlos of Spain and Princess Sophie of Greece in 1962. This jewel has never been worn since, but the present prince, Albert II, has lent it several times for various exhibitions.

A TREASURY OF WEDDING GIFTS

It was with the wedding of Prince Rainier and Grace Kelly im 1956 that the worldwide fascination with Monaco really began. Grace, a perfect Hollywood beauty, gave the principality the prestige and glamour it had previously lacked. Such was the impact of their union that presents poured in from every quarter – including jewels, of course. Pieces by Van Cleef & Arpels featured especially – a Daisy clip in platinum set with brilliant-cut diamonds and tiled with sapphires in the centre, given by an anonymous Monegasque, and a wide ribbon bracelet encrusted with diamonds from Monaco's Municipal Council. From the principality's National Council she received a triple diamond rivière of round and baguette diamonds created by the House of Cartier. In 2019, Princess Caroline's daughter, Charlotte Casiraghi – who never knew her grandmother – chose this exceptional jewel for her wedding to the film producer Dimitri Rassam.

Finally, the powerful Société des Bains de Mer, the state-owned Monegasque hospitality and gaming company, added to Grace's wedding gifts three Cartier brooches in gold and platinum, set with cabochon diamonds and rubies in the centre, which could be worn as a diadem attached to a gold frame or as a necklace. Grace wore this tiara on state visits to the Vatican in 1957 and to France in 1959, but more frequently wore the brooches, individually or as a pair, as part of her daytime outfits or as hair ornaments in her famous chignons. After her mother's death, Caroline would sometimes wear the brooches, though never as a diadem.

Cockerel brooch in gold and platinum adorned with aventurine, coral and diamonds, by Cartier, 1957; Hen brooch with pearls, coral, emerald and diamonds, Cartier, 1957; Poodle brooch, platinum and diamonds, Cartier, 1958.

THE FATE OF THE PRINCESS'S JEWELS

When out and about in Monaco, Grace opted for stylish but simple jewellery. Although she was seen several times wearing strands of pearls, either as a choker or as a sautoir, she never made them her trademark in the way Queen Elizabeth II did. Grace preferred heavy gold chains, most often sautoirs, Hermès gourmette chain bracelets and imposing ear clips, drawing her hair back with headbands to allow them to show. She also had a notable taste for animal brooches, which came from Cartier's exquisite bestiary of animal-themed designs: a bird, a hen, a scorpion and, above all, a poodle entirely covered with diamonds, in homage to Oliver, her own beloved black poodle. She was also fond of the duck-shaped clip created by Van Cleef & Arpels, in sapphires, diamonds and emeralds.

Since Grace's death in a car accident on 14 September 1982, aged only fifty-two, almost all her jewels have disappeared from view. Although Grace's elder daughter Caroline and, more rarely, her granddaughter Charlotte have occasionally worn a few pieces from her collection, her daughter Stéphanie has made it known that fine jewellery is not her thing. Likewise Charlène, Princess of Monaco since her marriage to Albert II in 2011, has never worn

This diadem by Cartier, known as the 'Bains de Mer' (opposite), was a wedding present to the princess from the powerful Société des Bains de Mer, the state-owned Monegasque hospitality and gaming company. The platinum and gold frame bears three round ruby cabochons crowned with floral motifs in diamonds, which are detachable and can be worn as clips (above) or as a necklace.

the jewels that belonged to the legendary mother-in-law she never met. Nevertheless, family tradition has demanded that the House of Van Cleef & Arpels create some exceptional pieces for her, including a diadem necklace consisting of 349 sapphires whose colour is graded into three hues, 833 round diamonds and a pear-shaped 4-carat diamond named Océan in homage to the seas around South Africa, the country where Charlène was in part raised and where she began her career as a competitive swimmer. The watery theme reappears in a diamond headpiece named Écume de diamants (Diamond Sea Foam), made by the House of Lorenz Bäumer for her civil wedding. This is made up of eleven pear-shaped diamonds, of which the most imposing weighs an astonishing 8 carats.

More than forty years after her death, Grace of Monaco remains a model of elegance and an undisputed icon. For a 2014 film in which the princess was played by Nicole Kidman, permission was obtained from the Grimaldi family to have the House of Cartier reproduce a few of the finest pieces from Grace's jewellery case, notably her engagement ring, the ruby and diamond cabochons, and the three-strand diamond necklace. These jewels, in turn, have become the stuff of legend.

This Cartier diadem in gold and platinum, featuring pear-shaped pearls, is one of the emblematic pieces in the Grimaldi jewellery collection. It was acquired by Princess Charlotte of Monaco in 1949, when her son Rainier ascended the throne. It has been worn many times by Princess Caroline.

The timeless Alhambra motif

In the 1970s, Grace of Monaco often wore, over knitwear or blouses, Alhambra sautoir necklaces by Van Cleef & Arpels, sometimes three at once — long gold chains interspersed with trefoil or quatrefoil motifs encrusted with various semiprecious stones, including malachite, onyx, mother-of-pearl, tiger's-eye and lapis lazuli. This flagship design was launched by Van Cleef & Arpels in 1968. These are simple and flexible pieces of fine jewellery, designed to be worn by a body in motion, unlike the formal jewellery of the past — a real revolution in jewellery design at the time, when society was itself undergoing many upheavals. The Alhambra motif, which appears throughout the collection, has become iconic. It of course brings to mind the famous fourteenth-century Moorish palace in Granada, Spain, where the quatrefoil appears in the palace's azulejos — tin-glazed painted tiles that were also used two centuries earlier in Syria and Byzantium. Most surprisingly, Alhambra jewellery, a deeply bourgeois symbol for five decades, has today been adopted by the young and fashionable, and especially by men. The basketball legend LeBron James, the British rapper Central Cee and the Spanish footballer Lamine Yamal, who plays for FC Barcelona, wear Alhambra pendants or bracelets, which have become a visible mark of success and ambition.

Grace attends a poetry reading in Edinburgh in 1979. She is wearing three of her numerous Alhambra sautoirs by the House of Van Cleef & Arpels.

'HEAVENS, MY JEWELS!'

Begum Om Habibeh

From Miss France 1930 to a queen of elegance, Begum Om Habibeh forged a life that might have come straight from the pages of *The Arabian Nights*. Her fabulous jewellery, too, was worthy of a fairy tale.

Yvette Labrousse, fourth wife of Aga Khan III, at a ball in New York, January 1957.
The press excitedly reported that she was wearing $1 million in jewellery.

Just after noon on 3 August 1949, a dark Cadillac drove away from Yakymour, a luxurious villa in the hills above Le Cannet, in the south of France. Seated to the chauffeur's right was a short, portly man with a tired face: Aga Khan III, one of the world's richest men. On the back seat was his wife, the young and statuesque Begum Om Habibeh, with her female personal assistant beside her. Between the two women was an elegant small trunk in red leather in which, under the lunch-time sandwiches, was a stack of caskets stamped with the names of the most famous Parisian jewellers. Among the velvet and satin nestled fabulous jewels, packed to adorn the begum in the coming days.

It was exactly 12.10pm when a car pulled out across the road, barring the way. Five men jumped out – a gang of criminals from Corsica and Marseille. One of them pointed his gun at the prince, while the two women were ordered to hand over the trunk and the jewels they were wearing. The begum is reputed to have loudly exclaimed: 'Heavens, my jewels!', and it was this legendary utterance that would serve as the inspiration for cartoonist Hergé's 1962 comic book *Les Bijoux de la Castafiore* (*The Castafiore Emerald*), part of *The Adventures of Tintin* series. The gangsters fled as the Aga Khan, undaunted, shouted contemptuously, 'You forgot the tip. Take this!' while holding out a wad of 220,000 francs. The attack lasted exactly two minutes, and the haul was worth some 213 million francs (£5.1 million or $6.9 million today). The following day the robbery was on the front page of every newspaper in France – the begum's jewellery had just become the stuff of legend.

On 18 August 1949, the Begum Om Habibeh was reunited with some of the jewels that had been stolen when her car was ambushed by armed robbers in Cannes two weeks earlier.

The Prince Aga Khan III and the Begum Om Habibeh in ceremonial dress, around 1950.

A fabulous necklace of pear-shaped pearls and pear-cut, marquise-cut and brilliant-cut diamonds, late 1960s.

A VERY TALL FIGURE WITH THE BEARING OF A QUEEN

Among the many jewels stolen was a ring set with an extraordinary diamond of 22 carats – 'marquise-cut', as the police report specified. This term derives from the jewel Louis XV commissioned for the Marquise de Pompadour: a stone whose fifty-five facets were said to perfectly reproduce the lips of the king's chief mistress. Just like Pompadour, whose original name was Jeanne-Antoinette Poisson, the Begum Om Habibeh began her life with neither title nor fortune – she was born Yvette Labrousse on 15 February 1906, in Sète, on the French Mediterranean coast. Her father, Adrien Labrousse, was a tram driver and his wife Marie a dressmaker, so no one would have predicted Yvette's illustrious future and marriage to a prince. She grew up in Cannes, lulled by the hum of the Rue d'Antibes, the city's fashionable shopping street. A daydreamer by nature, at school she tried to pass unnoticed, though her natural grace and great height – 1.83m (6ft) – made this impossible. On days when she was not at school she would snuggle up next to her father as he drove his tram, loving how it forged its winding way through the tumult of the city. Her father made fun of her taste for travel. 'Where will it get you?' he would ask her. To the ends of the earth – though neither of them knew it yet.

Yvette's diligence and eye for fashion convinced her parents that she would make a talented dressmaker. To give her the best chance of success, they moved to Lyon, where there was a thriving textile industry of cloth merchants and upmarket garment manufacturers. The tall, hard-working young trainee seamstress soon began modelling the creations of the studio that employed her. Her female colleagues, dazzled by her regal bearing and queenly stature, encouraged her to enter the Miss Lyon competition. Overcoming her natural shyness, Yvette agreed and won the title in 1929. Then, in 1930, she was

A 1957–8 Bulgari necklace in platinum set with turquoise gemstones and diamonds, worn by Begum Om Habibeh on 20 December 1958 (opposite). It is now in the collection of Prince Muhammad Shah Aga Khan.

crowned Miss France. From then on she travelled the world, wearing the creations of the greatest French fashion houses.

A journey to Egypt, eight years later, would turn the course of her life upside down. Still unmarried at the age of thirty-two, and still chaperoned by her parents, she met, at a gala dinner, His Highness Muhammad Shah Aga Khan III, 48th imam of the Nizari Isma'ili branch of Shia Islam. Although there was an age difference of twenty-nine years – and a height difference of more than a few centimetres – they fell in love. In the company of this infinitely courteous man, Yvette Labrousse would discover a whole new world: that of the Nizari Ism'ailis – fifteen million faithful in Africa and Asia, a branch of Islam descended from Fatima, daughter of the Prophet Mohammed, of which Aga Khan III had been the spiritual and political leader since the age of eight. But their fairytale was marred by furtive meetings and dashed hopes – for the Aga Khan was already married, and for six years his third wife, Andrée Carron, refused him a divorce. Only on 9 October 1944 could the couple finally be married.

109 KILOS OF GOLD AND PRECIOUS STONES

Yvette Labrousse, now converted to Islam, eagerly explored the customs and beliefs of her adopted people. She appeared dressed in Indian saris and wearing traditional jewellery. On the occasion of the Aga Khan's diamond jubilee, celebrated in Bombay on 16 March 1946, Yvette Labrousse – now Begum Om Habibeh – was made Mata Salamat ('Mother of Peace'), only the third woman in Islamic history to hold this supreme title. On that same day, before a crowd of followers, her husband sat down on one side of a gigantic pair of scales, while on the other side gold and precious stones were added until they were in perfect equilibrium – exactly 109 kg (240 lb).

The begum's jewellery collection was not unlike this shower of riches, though it would be many years before its extremely high quality would be gauged. On her death in 2000 – forty-three years after that of her husband – Sotheby's was entrusted with selling nineteen of her most remarkable jewels. One of the most significant pieces was an extravagant set

Begum Om Habibeh at the Prix de Diane in Chantilly on 9 June 1957. She is wearing earrings with clusters of pearls and diamonds and a five-strand necklace of cultured pearls.

An extravagant diamond necklace and matching earrings commissioned by Begum Om Habibeh at the end of the 1960s, doubtless made from the gems of a fringe necklace she owned. It is adorned with a profusion of pear-cut, marquise-cut, brilliant-cut and step-cut diamonds.

of pearls and diamonds, consisting of a platinum necklace decorated with flowers in yellow gold, set with marquise- and brilliant-cut diamonds and fringed with six enormous pearls, together with a matching bracelet and earrings. This parure was immediately bought by Aga Khan IV, then resold by his wife in 2016, five years after their divorce. Also featured was an astonishing brooch created by the French jewellery designer Pierre Sterlé for Chaumet. This jewel, named the Alexandre, depicted the King of Clubs from a deck of playing cards, whose body in mother-of-pearl and gold was highlighted by diamonds and rubies. His head, in hematite, was cut by Chaumet's master glyptician Robert Lemoine.

The begum was particularly fond of pearls: her favourite jewel was a marvellous necklace of five strands of fine pearls, which she most often wore with a brooch on a jacket collar. One of her favourites was in the shape of an exotic flower, set entirely with rubies and diamonds. This elegant woman could also boast possession not only of the purest, most colourless diamonds (D colour) – one of her most cherished necklaces had a profusion of pear-shaped and marquise diamonds – but also of a Harry Winston ring in which an emerald-cut diamond of 51.85 carats had pride of place. It sold for $2.7 million in 2000. However, a far more singular jewel was the begum's most beloved, doubtless because it was one of the last gifts from her husband. An ensemble of turquoises and diamonds by Bulgari designed in the 1950s, the necklace took the form of a broad bib, further enlarged in 1964 by Pierre Sterlé to include an exquisitely elegant star motif. She most famously wore these jewels at the legendary 'My Fair Lady' ball held by Hélène Rochas in Paris in 1965.

A PHARAONIC MAUSOLEUM

'I can only say that if a perfectly happy marriage is one in which there is a genuine and complete union and understanding, on the spiritual, mental, and emotional planes, ours is such,' wrote Aga Khan III of his wife in his memoirs published in 1954.[18] He died three years later, on 11 July 1957, to be succeeded, not by his son Aly Khan, but by his grandson Karim, whom he considered much more responsible. Aly's escapades as a society womanizer frequently allowed the press to have a field day, especially regarding his marriage to Hollywood actor Rita Hayworth. To house the body of her husband – who, she wrote, had allowed her to love the most beautiful things in life – the begum commissioned a sumptuous mausoleum at Aswan, on the banks of the Nile, whose construction she was able to oversee from the windows of the villa where the couple had lived for the three years before his death. Every day she had a red rose laid on his coffin, and she threw herself, heedless of the expense, into the charitable projects begun by her husband. In 1991, she set up the Om Habibeh Foundation, which to this day continues to work in support of children, access to education, and women's wellbeing.

During the last years of her life, in her villa at Le Cannet, the begum wore colourful saris and her famous pearl jewellery, worked passionately as a sculptor, continued to receive the great and the good, and made numerous donations to the municipality – which in return erected a bronze statue of her in one of its parks. Eventually, she became blind and died on 1 July 2000. On 15 November, her jewels were sold by Sotheby's, in aid of her good works.

Alexandre brooch, from the playing cards series created by Pierre Sterlé for Chaumet in 1965.

Begum Om Habibeh at a party in Paris, 3 November 1987.

ON THE ART OF SHINING IN SOCIETY

Brooke Astor

Thanks to her third marriage, the daughter of a naval officer became, at the age of fifty, the richest benefactor in New York. The queen of high society, Brooke Astor wore jewellery worthy of her status.

The American philanthropist Brooke Astor, photographed by Cecil Beaton in front of a painting entitled *The Astor Family*.

In 2005, something strange was going on at 778 Park Avenue. For months, Annette de la Renta, wife of the famous Dominican fashion designer, had not heard from her friend Brooke Astor – the woman who, just a short time before, had been the queen of New York. Accompanied by a friend, she eventually forced her way into Astor's immense duplex apartment, where she was met by the billionaire's visibly uncomfortable staff. Madam was barely presentable – her face slathered with make-up, her wig askew and her speech severely confused. A woman who had been impeccable, supremely regal, was now leaning on the glittering pommel of her cane. The housekeeper admitted to the two visitors that she herself had had to buy the pot of Nivea cream that had pride of place on the dressing table; not a penny remained to buy Madam Astor's precious ointments or luxury food, or to pay the person who walked her dogs, or her medical professionals. Although her fortune was still colossal – even at her advanced age of 103 – she no longer had full enjoyment of it, not since her diagnosis with Alzheimer's disease had been made. Her guardian, Anthony Dryden Marshall – her own son – had turned off the tap, blocking any expenditure necessary for her comfort. In this, he was joined by his latest wife, a shrewish woman who was as greedy as she was manipulative.

THE EMERALD, SYMBOL OF HOPE AND RENEWAL

Roberta Brooke Russell was born in 1902 – without a silver spoon in her mouth. There was as yet no promise of a fortune. Her father was a naval officer, an expatriate who took himself, his wife and their only daughter to China. Aged sixteen, she returned to the United States to marry the rising New Jersey politician John Dryden Kuser. Her husband's pockets might have been lined with gold, but his violent behaviour and alcoholism made her life impossible. She divorced Kuser, taking her only son with her, and embarked on a second marriage to Charles 'Buddy' Marshall, a foreign exchange dealer who was worth millions. She then went on to live it up, in the process neglecting her child, who would ever after hold it against her. In 1952, Brooke was suddenly widowed.

Brooke Astor wears her fabulous emeralds at the premiere of *La Traviata* in New York, 16 October 1989.

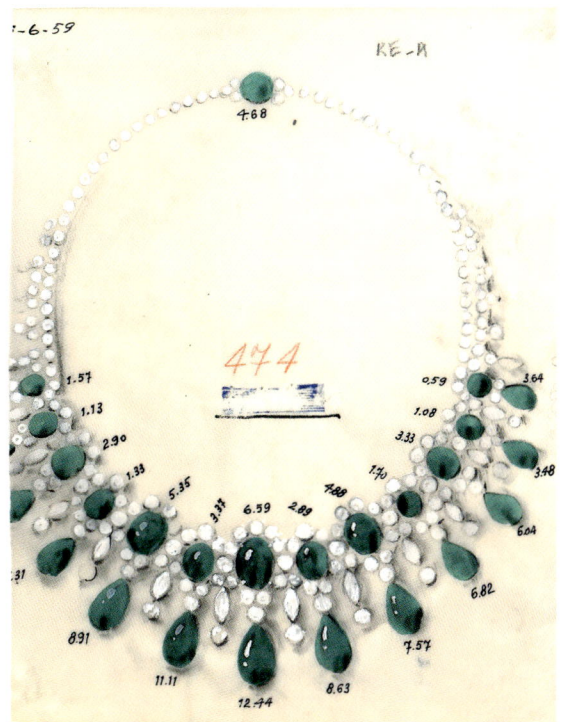

In 1959 the House of Bulgari made this sublime necklace of emeralds and diamonds set in platinum. It features twenty-seven Colombian cabochon emeralds — fourteen oval and thirteen pear-shaped — on a collarette of diamonds. It was the last gift from Brooke Astor's husband.

Brooke Astor 187

She was fifty years old and still wanted to shine in New York high society. She made a providential encounter in the shape of Mary Benedict Cushing, who was bent on only one thing: extracting a divorce from her husband, the extremely rich William Vincent Astor, to which he would only consent on the condition that she find him a new wife. The heir of one of the founding families of New York City was as insufferable as his fortune was vast, but Brooke felt she was up to the challenge and, even more, up to wearing the extravagant Verdura engagement ring that would seal their marriage agreement. This ring featured a cushion-cut emerald of 22.84 carats bordered by eight baguette-cut diamonds, and was worn by the bride the evening before her wedding, since it flattered, as she remarked, the colours of her flowing Balmain gown.

At the age of twenty, Vincent Astor was the most eligible man in America, his father having died in the *Titanic* disaster of 1912. He was also temperamental and quite an oddball, whom few people could handle. Nonetheless, he was unusual among his family in having a social conscience. Thus, for example, he demolished the squalid if highly profitable apartment buildings his family owned and replaced them with new ones with affordable rents, which were reserved for the poorest members of society – here was a billionaire who was almost a communist. But six years of marriage and one heart attack later, Brooke became the sole beneficiary of the Astor fortune, one of the most immense in America.

JEWELS FOR A UNIFORM

A few days before his death on 3 February 1959, Vincent Astor was staying in London, where he asked the Italian jeweller Giorgio Bulgari to join him for a meeting of the utmost importance: he wanted to give his wife an extraordinary gift. He opted for a set of twenty-seven Colombian cabochon emeralds

A set consisting of a brooch and earrings, set with emeralds, sapphires, and diamonds, Bulgari, 1963.
Starfish brooch from Tiffany & Co., by Jean Schlumberger, in 18 carat gold and diamonds.

– fourteen of them oval and thirteen pear-shaped – set into a small diamond necklace. The jewel was to be delivered to New York without fail by 30 March, Brooke's birthday. Vincent had been dead for only a few days when his widow received a photograph of the necklace and matching earrings from Bulgari, accompanied by an invoice and a note handwritten by her husband stating the place and date of delivery. This posthumous gift overwhelmed her, and in her memoirs she described how it had felt as though Vincent was sending her a message of encouragement from beyond the grave.

A widow in possession of a considerable fortune, and now also chief executive of the Vincent Astor Foundation, Mrs Astor became one of New York's most generous philanthropists, financing, to the tune of $200 million, the construction or renovation of schools, libraries and other public amenities. Her frail figure – emphasized by a Chanel suit, fascinator and heavy strands of pearls – was instantly recognizable. She liked to come to the aid of the poorest and distribute her money with style; indeed, it amused her: 'If I go up to Harlem or down to Sixth Street, and I'm not dressed up or I'm not wearing my jewellery, then the people feel I'm talking down to them. People expect to see Mrs. Astor, not some dowdy old lady, and I don't intend to disappoint them.'[19] And while she wore pounds of pearls and solid gold sautoirs around town, at gala evenings she was equally weighed down by the rarest of jewels, with a preference for diamonds and emeralds.

THE DIFFICULT END OF AN ERA

Haughty and strong-minded, Brooke Astor went into decline at the end of the 1990s. As her hundredth birthday approached, she had difficulty recognizing old friends, was often confused and could behave inappropriately. In 1999, during a dinner in the presence of Prince Charles and Camilla Parker-Bowles,

Vintage leaf and flower bracelet in diamonds and platinum, made by the House of Verdura in 1954. A present from Vincent Astor to his wife.

whose relationship had just been declared official, she even lost her manners: 'Your grandmother would be proud of you,' she let fly at the future duchess and queen, 'you're keeping this mistress business in the family' – an unsubtle reference to Alice Keppel, mistress of Edward VIII and a crime of lèse-majesté that created tension in the gathering.[20]

Fearing that his inheritance would elude him and go instead to the thousand charitable organizations his mother supported – too generously, in his view – Anthony Marshall decided to place his mother's fortune in a trust and in the process drastically tighten her expenditure. Accordingly, he dismissed the hairdresser, beautician, dog walker, chauffeur and chambermaid, before shutting up the old lady's favourite country home, Holly Hill in Westchester County, New York. Marshall had not reckoned, however, with the watchfulness of Annette de la Renta, Brooke Astor's most faithful friend, or with the mistrust of his own twin sons, who took legal action against their father for abuse of a vulnerable person. After numerous proceedings, Mrs de la Renta succeeded in having herself put in charge of the trust in co-operation with Brooke's two grandchildren, who were completely won over to her cause. Mrs Astor was thus able to get back to living a peaceful day-to-day life, until her death on 13 August 2007 at the age of 105. Two years later, her son was sentenced to three years in prison, on charges related to his handling of her finances, but was released after a year on medical grounds. He died in 2014 at the age of ninety, two years after his mother's collections were dispersed at auction.

Nine hundred lots were offered by Sotheby's, of which about sixty were pieces of *haute joaillerie*. As the 'last queen of New York' had intended, the proceeds were donated to museums, churches, schools, libraries and even a veterinary centre. Her engagement ring, featuring a superb emerald, attained ten times its estimate, $1.2 million, and her Bulgari emerald-and-diamond necklace sold for $686,500, almost three times its estimate. Brooke Astor would surely have rejoiced that people were paying top dollar for a piece of her legend.

Feather brooches transformed into clips.

Brooke Astor at the Plaza in New York, wearing a Verdura necklace in natural pearls, diamonds and platinum, 1996.

ABOUT THE AUTHOR

David Lelait-Helo is a novelist, essayist and biographer. As a child he dreamed of becoming a jeweller. He created collections of jewellery with plastic pearls and aluminium foil. Ever since he had the privilege, in 2011, of viewing the jewellery collection of Elizabeth Taylor, jewellery has been one of his great passions. With Line Renaud he is the author of the book *Mes années Las Vegas* [My Years in Las Vegas] (Éditions de La Martinière, 2018).

AUTHOR'S ACKNOWLEDGEMENTS

This book would never have seen the light of day without a child's gaze on the jewellery collections of his mother and grandmother. The jewels, whether real or imagined, of Grandma Mireille were, to me, a fantastic game – her sets impregnable castles, her sautoirs fascinating pieces of Meccano. I loved letting pearls run through my fingers, observing the sparkling of precious stones and the dance of jewels on skin. I dedicate this book to them.

Jewels are so intimate that they often struggle to reveal themselves. Putting this book together has not been simple – it has required flushing out secrets, exploring archives, defying censure. I would like to thank my editor, Isabelle Dartois for her constant commitment and tireless persistence, as well as her two talented assistants, Salomé Cozette and Lise Borget. A huge 'thank you' to Séverine Zorzetto, in charge of foreign rights at Éditions de La Martinière, for having found this book some homes from home.

I would like to thank the jewellery houses whose archives have been a precious resource. Thank you, too, to Bruno Barba at Sotheby's, and warm thoughts for Camille de Foresta, auctioneer and vice-president of Christie's France.

The literature of jewellery is extensive, and I have immersed myself in it with delight. I would like to pay tribute to the work of Henri Vever, especially on 19th-century French jewellery, as well as to the fascinating publications of the historian and journalist Vincent Meylan.

First published in Great Britain in 2025 by Mitchell Beazley, an imprint of Octopus Publishing Group Ltd
Carmelite House, 50 Victoria Embankment, London EC4Y 0DZ
www.octopusbooks.co.uk

An Hachette UK Company
www.hachette.co.uk

The authorized representative in the EEA is Hachette Ireland, 8 Castlecourt Centre, Dublin 15, D15 XTP3, Ireland (email: info@hbgi.ie)

First published in French under the title *Femmes aux bijoux*
© 2025, Éditions de La Martinière, a trademark of EDLM, 57 rue Gaston Tessier, 75019, Paris
English translation copyright © Octopus Publishing Group, 2025

Distributed in the US by Hachette Book Group
1290 Avenue of the Americas, 4th and 5th Floors
New York, NY 10104

Distributed in Canada by Canadian Manda Group
664 Annette St., Toronto, Ontario, Canada M6S 2C8

All rights reserved. No part of this work may be reproduced or utilized in any form or by any means, electronic or mechanical, including photocopying, recording or by any information storage and retrieval system, without the prior written permission of the publisher.

ISBN: 9781784729677
eISBN: 9781840919981

A CIP catalogue record for this book is available from the British Library.

Printed and bound in Slovenia.

10 9 8 7 6 5 4 3 2 1

For the English edition
Publishing Director: Alison Starling
Creative Director: Jonathan Christie
Senior Editor: Alex Stetter
Translator: Simon Jones
Copy Editor: Robert Anderson
Designer: Jeremy Tilston
Production Manager: Peter Hunt

FSC MIX Paper | Supporting responsible forestry FSC® C106600

PICTURE ACKNOWLEDGEMENTS

Every effort has been made to trace copyright holders. We would be grateful to be notified of any corrections for further editions.
[t: top, b: bottom, l: left, r: right, c: centre]

2, 153 ED/CVA/SOTHEBY'S/CAMERA PRESS/GAMMA-RAPHO; 4 Jean-Gabriel Domergue © Adagp, Paris, 2025; 7, 115rc, 116br, 156, 158l Nils Herrmann, Collection Cartier © Cartier; 8 Richard Drew/AP/SIPA; 10 Archives Photos/Photo de Paramount/Getty Images; 12, 54 Silver Screen Collection/Getty Images; 13l Marian Gérard, Cartier Collection © Cartier; 13r, 89tl, 135l Bridgeman Images; 14, 18, 20, 21, 86r Christie's via Bridgeman Images; 15, 24, 186 Ron Galella/Ron Galella Collection via Getty Images; 16 Express Newspapers/Hulton Archive/Getty Images; 17 reproduced with kind permission of the archives of David Webb; 19l, 25 Archives Cartier New York © Cartier; 19r Barry King/Liaison/Getty Images; 22tl, 68r © Christie's; 22bl, 22r, 44c, 44r, 72t, 72b, 74l, 74r, 119tl, 119tr, 119bl, 119br, 155l, 155r, 168l © Van Cleef & Arpels SA; 23c Barrella – Galerie Studio Orizzonte; 23bl, 187 Bulgari Historical Archives; 27 Fine Art Images/Heritage Images/Getty Images; 28, 33, 34, 66, 141tr, 141br, 142l, 142r, 143br © Christie's Images/Bridgeman Images; 29 Drew Angerer/Getty Images; 30l Nils Jorgensen/REX/Shutterstock/SIPA; 30r Nils Jorgensen/Cover Images/SIPA; 31 Sotheby's/Cover Images/SIPA; 32 © Mellerio; 37 Château de Versailles, Dist. RMN-Grand Palais/Christophe Fouin; 38 STILLS/GAMMA-RAPHO via Getty Images; 41 Jean-Pierre LELOIR/GAMMA-RAPHO; 43 Private collection, rights reserved; 44l, 51, 180l © AGIP/Bridgeman Images; 45 Farabola/Bridgeman Images; 46r, 46c, 46l, 110, 115r Marian Gérard, Collection Cartier © Cartier; 47 Cecil Beaton/CAMERA PRESS; 48 © Keystone-ATS; 53, 164r Photo by Sunset Boulevard/Corbis via Getty Images; 56 Sam Lévin/RMN-GP; 57 Sotheby's, London; 58 Sotheby's, New York; 59 © Roger-Viollet/Roger-Viollet; 61, 87, 92tl, 93, 113, 154 Bettman/Getty Images; 62 Studio Lipnitzki/Roger-Viollet; 65 Hulton-Deutsch Collection/Corbis/Corbis via Getty Images; 67 Photo by Doreen Spooner/Mirrorpix/Getty Images; 68l © William Spratling photo © Museum Associates/LACMA; 69 Mario De Biasi/Mondadori via Getty Images; 70 Sergio del Grande/Mondadori via Getty Images; 73 Keystone-France/Gamma-Keystone via Getty Images; 75 Getty Images; 76l Alain BUU/GAMMA-RAPHO via Getty Images; 76r Courtesy Beaussant Lefèvre/photo Philippe Sobert/Archives Bulgari; 77, 78r, 79l Courtesy Beaussant Lefèvre/photo Philippe Sobert; 78l Laurent SOLA/GAMMA-RAPHO via Getty Images; 79r photo by ARNAL-GARCIA/GAMMA-RAPHO via Getty Images; 81 Yousuf Karsh/CAMERA PRESS/GAMMA-RAPHO; 82 Everett Collection/Bridgeman Images; 83 Courtesy Bonhams; 84 Stan Honda/AFP; 85, 143tl, 143tr, 143cl, 143cr, 143bl, 188r © Tiffany & Co.; 86l Pat Greenhouse/The Boston Globe via Getty Images; 88 Tom Herde/The Boston Globe via Getty Images; 89tr Gérard Darel; 91 Photo by Chris Jackson – WPA Pool/Getty Images; 92tr George Pragnell Archives © Pragnell; 94l, 94r Archives Cartier London © Cartier; 95, 101, 105, 106, 122, 125, 127, 129, 134l Photo by Tim Graham Photo Library via Getty Images; 96 Serge Lemoine/Getty Images; 98 Peter Macdiarmid/Getty Images; 99 Express/Hulton Archive/Getty Images; 102, 104tr, 126 © Garrard; 103tl, 103tr © Royal Collection Enterprises Limited 2025|Royal Collection Trust; 104tl Universal History Archive/Universal Images Group via Getty Images; 107tl, 118l, 118r: © Archives Boucheron; 107tr Ranald Mackenzie/CAMERA PRESS/GAMMA-RAPHO; 109 Photo by Horst P. Horst/Condé Nast via Getty Images; 110, 134r, 161r, 177, 180r, 181 Courtesy Sotheby's; 112 Collections Chaumet (Paris) – © Chaumet; 114: Archives Cartier Paris © Pach Brothers studio; 115l, 115c, 116t, 116br, 120r, 150l, 150tr, 150br, 151, 158r, 159tl Archives Cartier Paris © Cartier; 116 Vincent Wulveryck, Collection Cartier © Cartier; 117 Jon Brenneis/Getty Images; 120l Lev Levitsky; 121 CAMERA PRESS/GAMMARAPHO; 124 Photo by Anwar Hussein/WireImage; 130l Photo by Hulton-Deutsch Collection/Corbis via Getty Images; 130r Photo by Samir Hussein/WireImage; 131 Photo by Kent Gavin/Daily Mirror/Mirrorpix/Getty Images; 132 SIPA; 133, 135r Photo by Julian Parker/UK Press via Getty Images; 137 © GrandPalaisRmn (musée d'Orsay)/Michel Urtado; 138l © Mellerio – Julien T. Hammon; 138r Collections Chaumet (Paris) – © Chaumet/Nils Herrmann; 139 © Archives Charmet/Bridgeman Images; 140 © GrandPalaisRmn (Domaine de Compiègne)/Franck Raux; 141l © GrandPalaisRmn (musée d'Orsay)/Stéphane Maréchalle; 144 © Iberfoto/Roger-Viollet; 145 source Bibliothèque nationale de France; 146l © GrandPalaisRmn (musée du Louvre)/Stéphane Maréchalle; 146r, 147t, 147b © Photo RMNGP/Stéphane Maréchalle; 148 Photo by Bachrach/Getty Images; 152 Photo by John Rawlings/Condé Nast via Getty Images; 157, 178, 180 Photo © AGIP/Bridgeman Images; 159tr, 159br Archives David Webb; 159bl Documentation Cartier Paris © Cartier; 160 Photo by Horst P. Horst/Condé Nast via Getty Images; 161l © David Behl 2011; 163 Gianni Bozzacchi – Archives du palais de Monaco – IAM; 164l, 166, 168l, 169l, 169c, 169r Geoffroy MOUFFLET – Archives du palais de Monaco – IAM; 165, 170l Photo by Carlos Alvarez/Getty Images; 167 Yousuf Karsh/CAMERA PRESS/GAMMA-RAPHO; 170r Rights reserved – Archives du palais de Monaco – IAM; 171 Georges Lukomski – Archives du palais de Monaco – IAM; 172 Photo by Alain BENAINOUS/GAMMA-RAPHO via Getty Images; 173 Photo by Anwar Hussein/Getty Images; 174 Photo by Ullstein Bild/Ullstein Bild via Getty Images; 176l KEYSTONE-FRANCE/GAMMA-RAPHO; 176r Photo by Apic/Bridgeman via Getty Images; 179, 187b, 188l Barrella – Studio Orizzonte Gallery; 182l Collections Chaumet (Paris) – © Chaumet/Rights reserved; 182r Collections Chaumet (Paris) – © Chaumet/Pauline Guyon; 183 Photo by Frédéric REGLAIN/GAMMA-RAPHO via Getty Images; 185 © Condé Nast; Royalty-Free; 186, 190l Photo by Ron Galella/Ron Galella Collection via Getty Images; 189 Photo by David Behl. Copyright Verdura; 190l © Antfarm Photography; 191 Copyright Verdura; rights reserved for other images.

NOTES

1. Elizabeth Taylor, *Elizabeth Takes Off* (New York: Putnam, 1988).
2. Elizabeth Taylor, with Ruth A. Peltason, *My Love Affair with Jewelry* (New York: Simon & Schuster, 2002).
3. Ibid.
4. Melvyn Bragg, *Richard Burton: A Life* (New York: Little, Brown & Co., 1989).
5. From a recording of an old interview in *Elizabeth Taylor: Rebel Superstar*, a three-part BBC documentary series, 2024
6. Taylor, *My Love Affair with Jewelry*
7. Ibid.
8. Ibid.
9. Ibid.
8. Sam Kashner and Nancy Schoenberger, *Furious Love* (London: JR Books, 2011).
9. Ibid.
10. Madame Campin, *Memoirs of the Court of Marie Antoinette, Queen Of France* (Boston, MA: L.C. Page & Co, 1900).
11. Thomas Carlyle, *The Diamond Necklace* (n.p., Houghton Mifflin, 1903).
12. Vincenzo Bellini, *Norma*, Act I, Scene iv.
13. Cited in Farah Nayeri, 'In Maria Callas's Career, La Scala Played a Major Role', *New York Times*, 20 January 2024.
14. Peter Evans, *Ava Gardner: The Secret Conversations* (New York: Simon & Schuster, 2013)
15. 'Ava Gardner', Encyclopedia of World Biography, ed. Tracie Ratiner, vol. 25 (Detroit: Gale, 2005).
16. Soraya Esfandiary-Bakhtiary, *Le Palais des solitudes* (Paris: Michel Lafon, 1991).
17. Patricia Volk, 'Oh, for those Pearls', *New York Times*, 10 March 1996.
18. Aga Khan III, Sir Sultan Muhammad Shah, *The Memoirs of the Aga Khan: World Enough and Time* (London: Cassell & Company, 1954), p. 274.
19. Quoted in Marilyn Berger, 'Brooke Astor, 105, Aristocrat of the People, Dies', *New York Times*, 14 August 2007.
20. Reported in Ed Pilkington, 'New York trial hears of "mistress" assault on Camilla', *Guardian*, 19 May 2009.